Unsung Heroes

Toronto forestry workers stand with their aerial tower trucks during a break in the action while in Kingston helping with emergency clean-up efforts after the 1998 Ice Storm.
— Courtesy City of Toronto

Unsung Heroes

Canadians Helping Canadians in the Face of Disaster

Nancy Loewen

Published in 2003 by
Construction Volunteers Canada,
Toronto, Ontario
nloewen@constructionvolunteers.org

Distributed by
Hushion House Publishing Ltd.
Toronto, Ontario

National Library of Canada Cataloguing in Publication Data

Loewen, Nancy (Nancy J.)
Unsung Heroes: Canadians helping Canadians in the face of disaster
ISBN 0-9732410-0-4

Disaster relief — Canada. 2. Volunteers — Canada. 3. Construction Volunteers Canada. 4. Canada. Canadian Armed Forces — Civic Action. 5. Canada. Armed Forces — Civic Action. I. Construction Volunteers Canada. II. Title.

HV555.C3L63 2003 363.3'48'0971 C2003-900320-5

Cover and text design: Heidy Lawrance Associates

Construction Volunteers Canada wishes to acknowledge the financial support of the Millennium Bureau of Canada.

Unsung Heroes is the Millennium Bureau of Canada project of Construction Volunteers Canada/Bénévoles Canadiens du Bâtiment under the name C.H.I.L.D. (Childrens' Humanity in Large Disasters). A portion of the royalties for *Unsung Heroes* will go to the communities represented by youth in this book.

Donations for Construction Volunteers Canada/Bénévoles Canadiens du Bâtiment can be made payable to Construction Volunteers Canada, and sent to:
Construction Volunteers Canada
Arthur Meighen Building
312-55 St. Clair Avenue
East Toronto, ON M4T 1M2

Map and legend on pp. ix–x reproduced with the permission of the Minister of Public Works and Government Services, 2002.

Printed and bound in Canada

Contact Construction Volunteers Canada at:
e-mail: nloewen@constructionvolunteers.org
Visit www.constructionvolunteers.org

Contents

A Word of Thanks

FIRST AND FOREMOST, I MUST THANK GOD, MY INSPIRATION FOR THIS BOOK. I see Christ in others when I travel to disaster sites to assist the needy.

My son, James — I am proud of the man you have become. You are strong and sensitive, honest and bright. Thank you for your support all these years.

I owe a debt of gratitude to my late parents, Josephine and Carmen (Mel) Masseo and Sam Grant, may you rest in peace. My four sisters, Val Sterling, Gail Wallrap, Doreen Menrad, and Barbara Ayearst, and their families have been a source of strength. My childhood friend, David Favalaro, who encouraged me to try difficult projects and was always there for me.

I would like to thank the Construction Volunteers Canada board of directors, for their support, guidance, and faith in my abilities.

To the volunteer tradesmen whose compassion makes our charity special in the eyes of Canadians: without your giving hearts, nothing could have been possible.

I owe thanks to the media who report on natural disasters. We rely on them heavily, and they were supportive in our appeal to tradesmen to volunteer after natural disasters. We are very grateful to the Canadian Forces who contributed stories and photos.

A tremendous thank you to the youth in schools across Canada who share their insightful anecdotes in this book, and to the teachers who guided them.

A large network of Canadians from various sectors contributed stories for this book; they are role models for all Canadians. They are to be commended for their compassion and leadership roles. I am constantly amazed and in awe of the indomitable spirit of Canadians when faced with devastation. I am proud to be living in this country.

❑ ❑ ❑

Construction Volunteers Canada/Bénévoles Canadiens du Bâtiment wish to acknowledge our Millennium partner, the federal government (Millennium Bureau of Canada), for their financial support and guidance; the Editors' Association of Canada; Heidy Lawrance Associates; Friesens Corporation; Jane Christmas, for her editorial contributions; Megan Bockus; Andrea Kennedy; and everyone else who helped with the book for generously giving their time, support, and donations. Finally, a warm thank you to all book participants for your patience and belief in this project. This charitable book was delayed because our publisher, one of the largest in Canada, became insolvent. This unfortunate situation did not deter us from fulfilling our obligation to the federal government and our commitment to the unsung heroes in this wonderful book.

Nancy Loewen (née Masseo)

September 2003

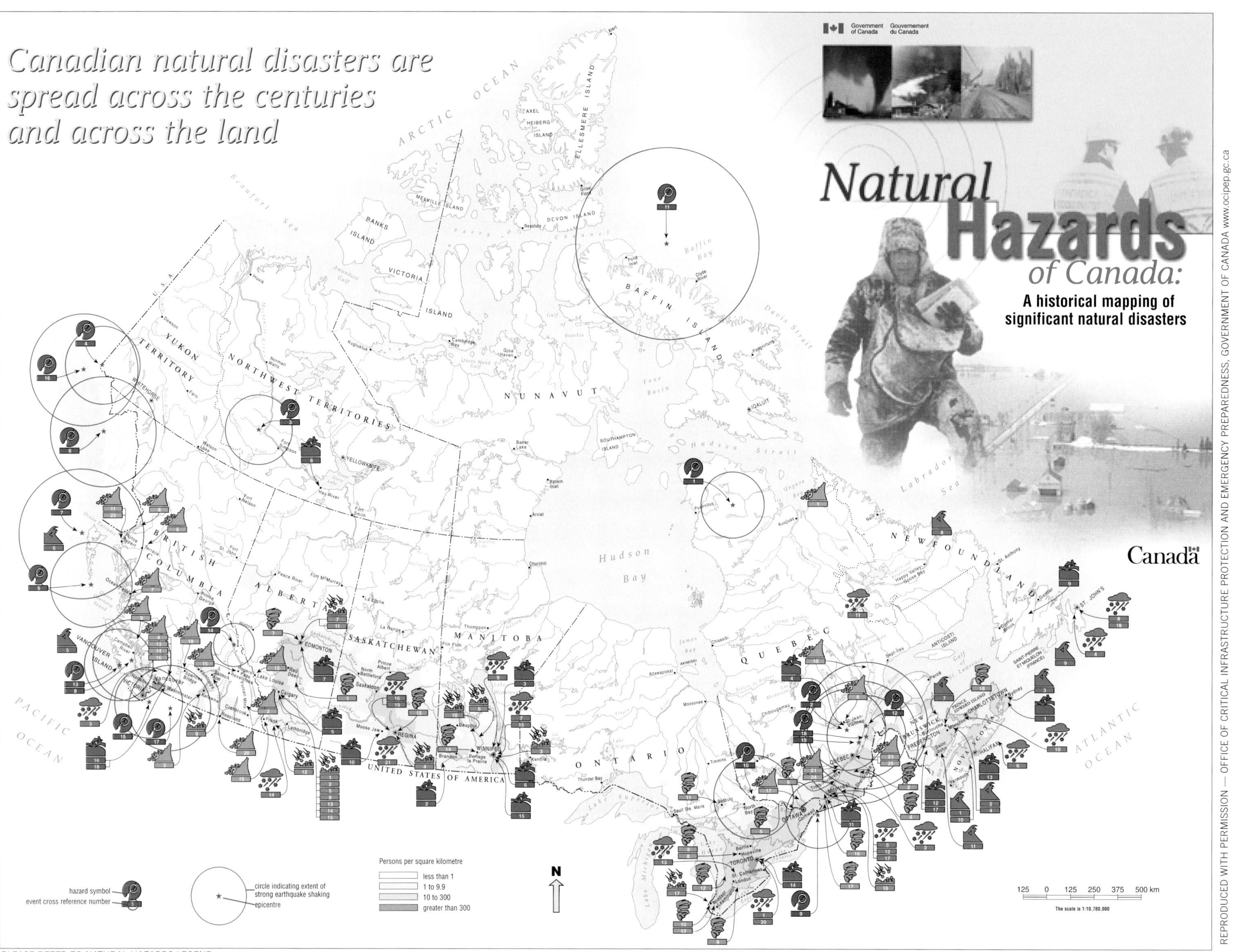
Canadian natural disasters are spread across the centuries and across the land
Government of Canada
Gouvernement du Canada
Natural Hazards of Canada:
A historical mapping of significant natural disasters
Canada
ARCTIC OCEAN
PACIFIC OCEAN
ATLANTIC OCEAN
Beaufort Sea
Baffin Bay
Davis Strait
Hudson Bay
Hudson Strait
Labrador Sea
ELLESMERE ISLAND
AXEL HEIBERG ISLAND
MELVILLE ISLAND
DEVON ISLAND
BANKS ISLAND
VICTORIA ISLAND
BAFFIN ISLAND
SOUTHAMPTON ISLAND
VANCOUVER ISLAND
YUKON TERRITORY
NORTHWEST TERRITORIES
NUNAVUT
BRITISH COLUMBIA
ALBERTA
SASKATCHEWAN
MANITOBA
ONTARIO
QUEBEC
NEWFOUNDLAND
NEW BRUNSWICK
PRINCE EDWARD ISLAND
NOVA SCOTIA
UNITED STATES OF AMERICA
U.S.A.
WHITEHORSE
YELLOWKNIFE
IQALUIT
EDMONTON
REGINA
WINNIPEG
TORONTO
OTTAWA
QUÉBEC
FREDERICTON
CHARLOTTETOWN
HALIFAX
ST. JOHN'S
VICTORIA
hazard symbol
event cross reference number
circle indicating extent of strong earthquake shaking
epicentre
Persons per square kilometre
less than 1
1 to 9.9
10 to 300
greater than 300
N
125 0 125 250 375 500 km
The scale is 1:10,780,000
PLEASE REFER TO NATURAL HAZARDS LEGEND

PLEASE REFER TO NATURAL HAZARDS MAP

Significant Disasters of the 19th and 20th Centuries

All damage figures are in year 2000 dollars

Icon | **Description**

Earthquakes

Earthquakes are perhaps the most dangerous of all natural hazards. They resulted in the loss of more than a million lives worldwide during the 20th century. Though they are not widely recognized as a major hazard, each year more than 50 earthquakes occur that are strong enough to be felt by Canadians. A further 1,400 smaller earthquakes are recorded each year by sensitive monitoring equipment. Both the West Coast and St. Lawrence Valley are at significant risk of a major earthquake.

1 **1989 Magnitude: 6.3**
Ungava Peninsula, QC / December / First earthquake in eastern North America confirmed to have produced surface faulting.

2 **1988 Magnitude: 6.0**
Saguenay region, QC / November / Felt in a 1,000-km radius from epicentre. Damage at Jonquière, Chicoutimi, La Baie, Québec and as far away as Montréal.

3 **1985 Magnitude: 6.9**
Nahanni region, NWT / December / Widely felt in NWT, Alberta and BC. A smaller event (magnitude 6.6) in the same area two months earlier triggered an avalanche containing five to seven million cubic metres of rock.

4 **1979 Magnitude: 7.2**
Yukon-Alaska border / February / Felt strongly in Canada, minor property damage in the Yukon.

5 **1970 Magnitude: 7.4**
South of Queen Charlotte Islands, BC / June / Widely felt.

6 **1958 Magnitude: 7.9**
Alaska-British Columbia border / July / People killed and much damage in Alaska. Parts of North-western B.C. and Southern Yukon strongly shaken.

7 **1949 Magnitude: 8.1**
Off the Queen Charlotte Islands, BC / August / Felt over a wide area of western North America. Canada's largest earthquake. Some damage on Queen Charlotte Islands.

8 **1946 Magnitude: 7.3**
Vancouver Island, BC / June / Widely felt. Extensive damage along the east coast of Vancouver Island; one person drowned.

9 **1944 Magnitude: 5.6**
Eastern Ontario-New York border / September / Widely felt. Damage at Cornwall, ON.

10 **1935 Magnitude: 6.2**
Quebec-Ontario border / November / Felt over much of eastern Canada. Minor damage at Temiscaming, QC and North Bay and Mattawa, ON.

11 **1933 Magnitude: 7.3**
Baffin Bay / November / Largest earthquake ever known north of the Arctic Circle.

12 **1925 Magnitude: 6.7**
Charlevoix-Kamouraska region, QC / March / Widely felt. Considerable damage along the St. Lawrence River near the epicentre and some damage at Québec, Trois-Rivières and Shawinigan.

13 **1918 Magnitude: 6.9**
Vancouver Island, BC / December / Widely felt, some minor damage near Estevan Point.

14 **1918 Magnitude: 6.0**
Revelstoke, BC / February / Felt in the BC interior.

15 **1909 Magnitude: 6.0**
Near south end of Strait of Georgia at a depth of about 65 km / January / Strongly felt in Canada, damage in U. S.

16 **1899 Magnitude: 7.9**
Yukon-Alaska border / September / First of three great earthquakes in this region in the space of eight days. Strong effects experienced in many parts of northern British Columbia and southern Yukon.

17 **1872 Magnitude: 7.4**
Washington-BC border / December / Widely felt.

18 **1870 Magnitude: 6.5**
Charlevoix-Kamouraska region, QC / October / Widely felt. Minor damage at Baie-Saint-Paul.

19 **1860 Magnitude: 6.0**
Charlevoix-Kamouraska region, QC / October / Widely felt. Minor damage at Rivière-Ouelle.

Floods

Floods are the highest costing natural disaster in Canada in terms of property damage. They can occur in any region, in the countryside or in cities, at virtually any time of the year. They have affected hundreds of thousands of Canadians. Most flooding occurs when the flow of water in a river or stream exceeds its channel. Floods also occur along the shoreline of lakes and oceans when water rises after high runoff, storm surge or the hammering of waves.

1 **1999 Estimated damage: $12 million**
Maritime Provinces / September / Record rainfall caused by remnants of tropical storm Harvey and Hurricane Gert flooded Oxford, NS with 200 mm rain in 24 hours. Moncton, NB was forced to evacuate 30 seniors from a residence and 15 families and 10 metre whitecaps smashed the breakwater in Lord's Cove, NF, and wharves in Placentia Bay and St Brides.

2 **1999 Estimated damage: $103 million**
Melita, MB / April / The flooding of the Souris River washed out roads and damaged bridges in rural areas, and made 800,000 hectares of farmland unseedable.

3 **1997 Estimated damage: $815 million**
Manitoba's Red and Assiniboine River valleys / May / Thousands of volunteers, including residents, military personnel and volunteers worked together for over a month to battle spring floodwaters and evacuate 25,000 people from the dozens of affected communities.

4 **1996 Estimated damage: $1.5 billion**
Saguenay River valley, QC / July / Ten people died and 15,825 people were evacuated when floodwaters washed out thousands of homes, businesses, roads and bridges. The flooding was caused by a sustained downpour of 290 mm of rain over 36 hours.

5 **1995 Estimated damage: $156 million**
Southern Alberta / June / Heavy rain and melt water led to flooding of Oldman and Saskatchewan rivers. Roads, property, riverbanks, agricultural land and 20 bridges were damaged. 250 homes were flooded.

6 **1993 Estimated damage: $406 million**
Winnipeg, MB / July to August / City of Winnipeg declared disaster area after prolonged heavy rainfall and 3 thunderstorms. Sewer backups, homes damaged, power lines down, agricultural land and infrastructure damaged. Wettest summer in 120 years.

7 **1986 Estimated damage: $66.9 million**
Edmonton, AB and Prince Albert, SK / July / Flood was the highest since 1915.

8 **1985 Compensation of $1.1 million**
Northwest Territories / May / Spring runoff and ice jams flooded the west channel area of Hay River.

9 **1983 Estimated damage: $61.6 million**
Newfoundland / January / A rainstorm, snowmelt and a rapid ice break-up led to severe flooding in the Exploits and Gander River basins. Damage included the partial destruction of the dam and powerhouse at Bishop's Falls.

10 **1974 Estimated damage: $23.4 million**
Saskatchewan / April / Runoff from a heavy snowpack flooded the Qu'Appelle River basin and drove the Moose Jaw River to a historical high. In Moose Jaw, 60 city blocks were under water; bridges and dams were damaged.

11 **1974 Estimated damage: $359 million**
Quebec / May-June / Floods struck hundreds of towns, with the Ottawa River basin and Montréal region hardest hit. Caused by unusually wet spring and excessive snowmelt, total damages were $359 million. Over 1000 homes and 600 cottages were flooded, and 10,000 people evacuated.

12 **1973 Estimated damage: $127 million**
New Brunswick / April / A frontal storm in the northern and central parts of the province unleashed the largest flood since records have been kept. Damages to Fredericton area and farmland accounted for about 60 percent ($77.8 million) of total.

13 **1956 Estimated damage: $213.8 million**
Nova Scotia / January / Snowmelt, rain and ice jams caused extensive province-wide damages including the destruction of more than 100 bridges. Tropical storms also have wreaked havoc, such as Hurricane Beth in August 1971 that inflicted $129.5 million in estimated damages.

14 **1954 Estimated damage: $1.03 billion**
Ontario / October / Hurricane Hazel induced the worst flooding in the Toronto area in more than 200 years. The toll included 81 dead and more than 20 bridges destroyed.

15 **1950 Estimated damage: $1.09 billion**
Manitoba / April-May / The 51-day Red River flood in and around Winnipeg was caused by snowmelt and heavy rain and caused major damage despite extensive dyking. One person died, and 107,000 were evacuated.

16 **1948 Estimated damage: $427 million**
British Columbia / May / Fraser River rose to within one foot of the 1894 level and flooded more than 22,000 hectares.

17 **1923 Estimated damage: $75 million**
New Brunswick / April-May / The flood was caused by snowmelt, heavy rain, ice and log jams and was significant in all parts of the province. Two lives were lost.

18 **1894 Estimated damage: Unknown**
British Columbia / The greatest Fraser River flood in the past century occurred when the floodplain was sparsely populated and undeveloped. Had the same flood struck the lower Fraser in 2000, it could have caused damages of $7.5 billion.

Tornadoes

Tornadoes are unmistakable rotating columns of high velocity wind that brings devastation to anything in their path. They are difficult to predict. They move quickly and can leave a wide swath of destruction. At other times the tornado is small, touching down sporadically and leaving a skipping damage path. In either case they can uproot trees, flip cars and demolish houses. Canada probably gets more tornadoes than any other country with the exception of the United States. Southwestern Ontario and parts of the southern Prairies are most often struck.

1 **2000 Fatalities: 12, 140 injured**
Pine Lake, AB / August / A 300-km/hr tornado hit a campground. 1,000 people were displaced, recreational vehicles destroyed, and there were $12 million in damages.

2 **1999 Fatalities: 1, 4 injured**
Drummondville, QC / July / Roof ripped from 20 homes, 60 others damaged, 200 people evacuated and $12.4 million in damages.

3 **1996 Fatalities: 9 injured**
Grey, Wellington and Dufferin Counties, ON / April / Two F3 tornadoes caused $12.3 million in damage.

4 **1994 Fatalities: 4 injured**
Aylmer, QC / August / 1000 people had to be evacuated after this F3 tornado caused $14.4 million in damages to 385 homes and other buildings.

5 **1991 Fatalities: 15 injured**
St. Lawrence Valley, QC / August / Maskinongé was hardest hit among three communities with 60 percent of buildings damaged, lost electricity, telephone and drinking water, $25.4 million in damages.

6 **1990 Fatalities: 6 injured**
Southern Ontario / August / Several tornadoes were spawned by this storm front, causing $1.2 million in damages to crops and buildings.

7 **1987 Fatalities: 27, 300 injured**
Edmonton, AB / July / Thousands homeless, damage of $662.3 million.

8 **1985 Fatalities: 12, 155 injured**
Hopeville to Barrie, ON / May / More than 1,000 buildings damaged at a cost of $301 million.

9 **1975 Fatalities: 3, 59 injured**
Trois Rivières, QC / July / 918 people had to be relocated after this late afternoon tornado damaged 75 homes and caused $34.6 million in damages.

10 **1974 Fatalities: 9, 30 injured**
Windsor, ON / April / Damage of $1.8 million.

11 **1970 Fatalities: 6, 200 injured**
Sudbury, ON / August / Damage of $45.5 million.

12 **1953 Fatalities: 7, 40 injured**
Sarnia, ON / May / 500 people had to be evacuated after this tornado caused $59.7 million in damages.

13 **1946 Fatalities: 17, hundreds injured**
Windsor to Tecumseh, ON / June / Damage conservatively estimated at $9.7 million.

14 **1922 Fatalities: 5, and scores injured**
Portage la Prairie, MB / June / Damage of $20 million.

15 **1912 Fatalities: 28, hundreds injured**
Regina, SK / June / Damage of $45 million.

16 **1892 Fatalities: 6, 26 injured**
Sainte-Rose, QC / June

17 **1888 Fatalities: 11, 14 injured**
Lancaster, ON to Saint-Zotique, QC / August / Extensive property damage.

18 **1879 Fatalities: 7, 10 injured**
Buctouche, NB / August / Extensive damage left 25 families homeless.

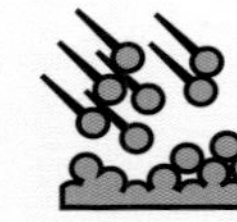

Hail forms in the cores of thunderstorms. Water vapour in warm, rapidly rising air masses (convection currents), condenses into water at higher, cooler altitudes, producing heavy rain showers. If it is cold enough, ice crystals can form around minute particles, such as dust whipped up from the ground. These increase in size as more water freezes on to their surfaces. When the ice pellets are too heavy for the ascending air currents to lift, they fall as hail. They may become larger, heavier and more damaging if they collect more water on the way down.

1 **1998 Estimated damage: $63.4 million**
Calgary, AB / July / Two separate hailstorms hit the city. High winds of 100 km/h accompanied storm. Flooding and hail damage caused $63.4 million in damages.

2 **1996 Estimated damage: $303 million + $87.8 million for second hailstorm**
Calgary, AB / July / Hailstorm caused heavy flooding and extensive damage to property and automobiles. A second hailstorm six days later added another.

3 **1996 Estimated damage: $151 million**
Winnipeg, MB / July / Tennis ball sized hail smashed property, crops, gardens and windows. A tornado accompanied high winds.

4 **1995 Estimated damage: $13.3 million.**
Regina, SK / August

5 **1995 Estimated damage: $74.6 million**
Calgary, AB / July

6 **1995 Estimated damage: $28 million**
Southern Manitoba / July

7 **1995 Estimated damage: $34.5 million**
Edmonton, AB / July

8 **1994 Estimated damage: $30 million**
Southern Alberta / June

9 **1994 Estimated damage: $11 million**
Salmon Arm, BC / August

10 **1994 Estimated damage $14.3 million**
Southern Manitoba / August / Two separate hail storms rolled through Southern Manitoba communities and farmlands.

11 **1993 Estimated damage: $21 million.**
Edmonton, AB / July

12 **1992 Estimated damage: $38.5 million.**
Calgary, AB / July

13 **1991 Estimated damage: $884 million**
Calgary, AB / September / A 30-minute thunderstorm hit Calgary with downpours and golf-ball-sized hail. Homes were flooded and had windows broken.

14 **1990 Estimated damage: $22 million**
Calgary, AB / July / Hail storm bombarded Calgary and surrounding region.

15 **1988 Total claims: $60.3 million.**
Calgary, AB / August / A thunderstorm produced up to 5 cm. hailstones, in addition to 40-200 mm of rain. Flooding and hail damaged 3,000 properties and 2,000 automobiles.

16 **1986 Estimated damage: $15.5 million**
Montréal, QC / May / Hail up to 8 cm. in diameter fell onto the city.

17 **1985 Estimated damage: $24.5 million**
Windsor to Leamington, ON / May / Five people were killed when golf-ball sized hailstones smashed greenhouses, damaged property and flattened crops.

Landslides and snow avalanches have resulted in more than 600 deaths in Canada since 1840, and have caused billions of dollars in damage. These mass movements of soil, rock or snow occur in all parts of the country, in mountains and flatlands, and usually without warning. Hazards include the impact of rapidly moving debris, the collapse of ground beneath a structure, and secondary effects such as river damming and landslide-generated waves.

1 **1999 Fatalities: 9, 25 injured**
Kangiqsualujjuaq, QC / January / Tonnes of snow cascaded down a cliff and knocked out a school gymnasium wall. Victims were inside participating in a New Year's Eve party. Ten other buildings were evacuated.

2 **1991 Fatalities: 9**
Purcell Mountains, BC / March / Snow avalanche struck helicopter skiing party

3 **1990 Fatalities: 7**
Joe Rich and Southern BC / June / Debris avalanche and mudslides caused by heavy rains closed 3 highways and reduced TransCanada highway, eight homes destroyed in four communities by mudslides.

4 **1981 Fatalities: 9**
M-Creek Bridge, Highway 99, BC / October / Cars plunged into creek after debris flow had destroyed bridge during heavy rains.

5 **1971 Fatalities: 7**
North Route Cafe, BC / Snow avalanche destroyed roadside café.

6 **1971 Fatalities: 31**
St-Jean-Vianney, QC / May / Rapid retrogressive flowslide in Leda Clay swept away 40 homes.

7 **1965 Fatalities: 7**
Ocean Falls, BC / January / Slush avalanche/debris flow caused by melting snow struck community.

8 **1965 Fatalities: 26**
Granduc Mine, BC / February / Snow avalanche struck sleeping quarters of mining camp.

9 **1964 Fatalities: 5**
Ramsay Arm, BC / September / Debris flow caused by heavy rains struck logging camp.

10 **1962 Fatalities: 8**
Rivière Toulnustouc, QC / December / Workers killed by landslide in marine clay caused by blasting.

11 **1957 Fatalities: 7**
Prince Rupert, BC / November / Debris avalanche triggered by heavy rains buried 3 houses.

12 **1955 Fatalities: 7**
Mount Temple, Lake Louise, AB / July / Inexperienced climbers swept away by snow avalanche.

13 **1921 Fatalities: 37**
Britannia Beach, BC / October / Outburst flood caused by breach of landslide dam swept away more than 50 houses.

14 **1915 Fatalities: 56**
Jane Camp, BC / March / Rock avalanche from above portal of mine swept into mining camp.

15 **1910 Fatalities: 62**
Rogers Pass, BC / March / Workmen clearing snow from previous avalanche on CP tracks buried by second avalanche.

16 **1909 Fatalities: 22**
New Westminster, BC / November / Slump of railway embankment; train derailed.

17 **1908 Fatalities: 33**
Notre-Dame-de-la-Salette, QC / April / Landslide in Leda Clay into Lièvre River caused a wave containing blocks of ice, which destroyed homes.

18 **1905 Fatalities: 15**
Spences Bridge, BC / August / Landslide into Thompson River caused wave, which swept victims away.

19 **1903 Fatalities: 70**
Frank, AB / April / Rock avalanche buried the coal mining town of Frank.

20 **1897 Fatalities: 7**
Red Mountain, BC / Debris flow struck railway camp.

21 **1895 Fatalities: 5**
Saint-Luc-de-Vincennes, QC / Landslide in Leda Clay.

22 **1891 Fatalities: 35**
North Pacific Cannery, BC / Debris flow or flood caused by breach of landslide dam after heavy rains.

23 **1889 Fatalities: 45**
Québec, QC / Rockslide onto houses on Champlain Street.

24 **1877 Fatalities: 5**
Sainte-Geneviève-de-Batiscan, QC / Landslide in Leda Clay

25 **1841 Fatalities: 32**
Québec, QC / Rockslide onto houses on Champlain Street.

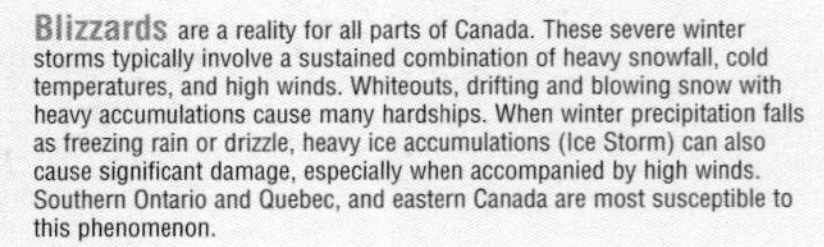

Blizzards are a reality for all parts of Canada. These severe winter storms typically involve a sustained combination of heavy snowfall, cold temperatures, and high winds. Whiteouts, drifting and blowing snow with heavy accumulations cause many hardships. When winter precipitation falls as freezing rain or drizzle, heavy ice accumulations (Ice Storm) can also cause significant damage, especially when accompanied by high winds. Southern Ontario and Quebec, and eastern Canada are most susceptible to this phenomenon.

1 **1999 Precipitation: 118 cm. of snow**
Southern Ontario / January / Less than 2 weeks after Toronto was dumped with 40 cm of snow another major storm dumped 78 cm of snow on the city, bringing the total to 118 cm. The storm shut down parts of the Toronto's transit system and left thousands stranded. All of Southern Ontario's 7.1 million people were affected and damages were estimated at $122 million.

2 **1998 Precipitation: 50-100 mm. freezing rain**
Ontario to New Brunswick / January / Ice storm hit a corridor extending through Kingston, Ottawa, Montréal, Montérégie area south and east of Montréal, and on into New Brunswick, causing massive power outages. 200 Quebec and 57 Ontario communities declared a disaster with almost 5,000,000 people left without power. Damage estimates are near $7 billion.

3 **1996 Precipitation: 100 cm. of snow**
Southwestern BC / December / An unusually heavy snowfall brought traffic and emergency response service to a standstill in the areas of Victoria, the Fraser Valley, and some parts of Vancouver. Damage estimated at $214 million.

4 **1994 Precipitation: Wet snow, sleet, 168 km/h winds**
Avalon, NF / December / A severe storm caused build-up of up to 15 cm in diameter on wires causing major damage to the transmission and distribution systems on the Avalon, Burin and Bonavista Peninsulas.

5 **1994 Precipitation: 25 cm. of snow, 70 km/h winds, -18°C**
Montréal region, QC / January / Snowfall and high wind combined to produce almost zero visibility, causing major highway accidents and at least 6 deaths. Power failures left about 6,000 homes in Montréal without heat or light overnight.

6 **1993 Precipitation: Snow, high winds**
East Coast / March / A severe blizzard caused by a mid-latitude cyclone moved up the North American East Coast eventually claiming more than 240 lives; at one point over 3 million people were left without electricity. Damage estimated at $20 million.

7 **1986 Precipitation: 30 cm. of snow, 90 km/h winds**
Winnipeg, MB / November / A major storm in Winnipeg produced severe blowing snow, zero visibility and 2 dead.

8 **1984 Precipitation: Freezing rain**
St. John's, NF / April / 200,000 people of the Avalon Peninsula were left without heating and lighting for days after overhead electrical wires snapped from the weight of a 15 cm. of ice build-up.

9 **1983 Precipitation: Freezing rain**
Prairie Provinces / March / The ice storm forced Winnipeg International Airport to close for two days, toppled several large television towers and caused other extensive damage.

10 **1982 Precipitation: 60 cm. of snow, 80 km/h winds**
Prince Edward Island / February / Islanders were marooned for five days in a crippling blizzard; winds whipped snow into 7-m. drifts.

11 **1982 Precipitation: Snow, 130 km/h winds, -30°C**
Labrador City, NF / January / 2000 people were evacuated from their homes; three people died from extreme cold; power lines snapped from the weight of ice; the city was left without power; a State of Emergency was issued by the mayor.

12 **1971 Precipitation: 47 cm. of snow, 110 km/h winds**
Montréal, QC / April / The city's worst snowstorm produced huge drifts. Electricity was cut for 2-7 days.

13 **1968 Precipitation: Freezing rain and wet snow**
Southern Ontario / January / Three days of freezing rain and wet snow caused widespread power failures, school closures, cancellations or disruption of services, the collapse of several buildings, and highway blockages.

14 **1967 Precipitation: 175 cm. of snow, 100 km/h winds**
Southern Alberta / April / A series of intense winter storms dropped record snow onto southern Alberta. Thousands of cattle, unable to forage for food in the deep snow, perished on the open range.

15 **1966 Precipitation: 35 cm. of snow, 120 km/h winds**
Winnipeg, MB / March / The storm paralyzed the city for two days.

16 **1964 Precipitation: Snow, 90 km/h winds**
Southern Prairies / December / Referred to as the "Great Blizzard", it produced heavy snows, high winds and -34°C temperatures. Three people froze to death and thousands of animals died.

17 **1961 Precipitation: Freezing rain, 120 km/h wind gusts**
Montréal, QC / February / This ice storm caused heavily loaded utility wires to snap; a week after the storm, parts of the city were still left without electricity. Damage estimated at $40.9 million.

18 **1959 Precipitation: Snow, high winds**
St. John's, NF / February / Described as the province's worst snowstorm, it claimed six lives, left 70,000 without electricity, and blocked roads with 5 m drifts.

19 **1947 Precipitation: Snow, high winds**
Prairie Provinces / January / A blizzard raged for 10 days from Winnipeg to Calgary; the railway called it the worst storm in Canadian rail history; one train was buried in a snowdrift 1 km long and 8 m deep.

20 **1944 Precipitation: 57 cm. of snow over two days**
Toronto, ON / December / A blizzard accompanied by strong winds caused huge drifts, which paralysed the city for days. In all, 21 people died.

21 **1941 Precipitation: Snow, 100 km/h winds**
Southern Prairie provinces / March / A severe blizzard producing a storm called an "Alberta Low" lasted 7 hours and caused 76 deaths in the southern parts of the Prairie provinces and the northern U.S.

Tsunamis and Storm Surges are caused by different events but both result in flooding and damage to coastal areas. **Tsunamis** are immense sea waves (10 metres or more), which are produced by underwater events such as earthquakes, mudslides and volcanic eruptions. They start out small in the open seas but amplify in size as they reach shallow water. **Storm Surges** are elevated sea levels produced by intense marine low pressure systems. Storm Surges at times of high tides can lead to coastal flooding and are often accompanied by large ocean waves.

1 **2000 Storm Surge: 1.6 metres above high tide mark**
North shore of Prince Edward Island and the Gulf of St. Lawrence coast of New Brunswick / October / The remains of a tropical storm hit the Gulf of the St. Lawrence with wind gusts of 120 km/h, building ocean waves of 7-11 metres and causing massive damage to coastal infrastructure.

2 **2000 Surge Size: 1.2 - 2.0 metres**
Maritime Provinces / January / An intense winter storm hit the Maritimes during a run of very high tides. The storm was accompanied by up to 70 centimetres of snow, high winds and -40 degrees centigrade wind chill. The storm surge caused coastal flooding in the Gulf of St. Lawrence affecting Prince Edward Island, New Brunswick and Nova Scotia, exceeding previous records. In places, the storm surge forced winter ice onto shorelines. Damages were estimated at $20 million.

3 **1983 Surge Size: 0.76 to 1.5 metres**
Cape Breton Island, NS / October / Water levels rose 0.76 to 1.5 metres above normal high water mark. Storm surge flooded coastal highways, destroyed 30 fishing boats and thousands of lobster traps.

4 **1976 Surge Size: 1.6 metres**
Bay of Fundy, NS and NB, February / Hurricane force winds accompanied the Groundhog Day storm of February in the Maritimes. Hardest hit was southwestern Nova Scotia and southern New Brunswick with coastal flooding and extensive damage to wharves, coastal buildings, boats and vessels. Power and communications lines were also knocked out. Damage was estimated in the tens of millions of dollars.

5 **1964 Tsunami Size: 2.4 to 6 metres**
British Columbia outer coast / March / A magnitude 8.5 earthquake in Alaska caused a 2.4-metre wave at Tofino. Run-up was higher in many areas. Amplitude in Port Alberni was over six metres damaging 320 buildings and causing $8.4 million in damage.

6 **1960 Tsunami Size: 1.2 metres**
British Columbia's outer coast / A magnitude 9.5 earthquake in Chile caused a 1.2-metre wave at the Tofino tide gauge. Run-up was higher in many areas. There was damage to log booms along the western coast of Vancouver Island and in the Queen Charlotte Islands.

7 **1959 Surge Size: Unregistered**
New Brunswick / June / Hurricane-type storm with heavy rainfall and storm force winds hit New Brunswick and Prince Edward Island. It resulted in the death of many fishermen in the Gulf of St. Lawrence, who did not have time to get back to shore before the storm hit. The winds and ocean waves at sea were the most damaging aspects of the event but high tides and coastal flooding was reported in New Brunswick.

8 **1951 Surge Size: Unregistered**
Newfoundland coastline / December / A severe storm with high wind velocities caused a storm surge and forced the evacuation of 600 people from along the Newfoundland coastline.

9 **1929 Tsunami Size: 5 metres**
Burin Peninsula, NF / November / A 7.2 magnitude earthquake in the Atlantic Ocean, south of Newfoundland generated a tsunami, which drowned 27 people and destroyed houses, boats and docks on the Burin Peninsula.

10 **1873 Surge size: Unregistered**
Gulf of St. Lawrence coast of New Brunswick / August / Hurricane caused many sunken ships and fatalities in the Gulf of St. Lawrence due to sudden windstorm. There was extensive flooding and coastal damage in southwestern Gulf of St. Lawrence.

11 **1869 Surge size: 1.2 - 2.1 metres**
Bay of Fundy, NS and NB / October / The Saxby Tide, which accompanied the Saxby Gale, caused major flooding along the Bay of Fundy and overtopped or destroyed the dykes that protected the reclaimed salt marshes. The storm caused damage to wharves, coastline buildings, boats and vessels. A number of fatalities were associated with the storm, which were caused by ships sinking at sea and people drowning in the coastal flood.

PLEASE REFER TO NATURAL HAZARDS MAP

Introduction

ON A COLD DAY IN JANUARY 1998, I SAT IN MY WARM, COZY LIVING ROOM watching the coverage of the Ice Storm on CBC television news. Some Quebecers were being interviewed in an Ice Storm "shelter." I thought to myself, how can there still be power outages in this day and age? A mother with babe in arms was crying because she couldn't return home. A few days later, I watched an electrician sobbing in what became known as the "Black Triangle," the area in which 40,000 people were engulfed in darkness. He was distressed because he couldn't work fast enough to help his community. I sat there and cried. Little did I know at the time that this would be the beginning of a new life for me. I would become a full-time volunteer, a humanitarian.

After three days of anguish, I got up from my comfortable couch, said a prayer, and shut off my own furnace. I felt it was essential that I try to feel the pain of the victims of the Ice Storm. After two days of extreme cold, worrying if my pipes would freeze, wearing many layers of clothing, I began to understand. Then I knew what I had to do. I told my son, James, that I was travelling to Quebec to help our fellow Canadians. He told me that the Salvation Army and Canadian Red Cross were providing aid. He asked me what I could possibly contribute. I said, "I'll hold their hands, give them hugs, and encourage them to laugh." I wasn't worried about the dangers the Ice Storm presented. I was only worried about the fact I couldn't speak French. I only had my high school French, so my pronunciation was lousy.

THE WEATHER NETWORK

I called the emergency response departments of the Ontario and Quebec governments. In addition, I also called the media and appealed to tradesmen to volunteer their time and donate the use of their trucks. I am not a construction worker, nor did I, at the time, have any experience coordinating large groups of people, so I wasn't sure if the tradesmen would listen to me. All I knew was that this compassion I felt was real and I had to find people who felt the same way.

To my amazement the tradesmen returned my calls. I sent the first group of volunteers, from Toronto, to Montreal. They would help clean up Mt. Royal Park. The second group of volunteers were tree specialists from Al Miley & Associates. I sent them to Goulburn Township, south of Ottawa, Orangeville, Ontario as well as to Oka and St. Placide, Quebec. They appeared on CBC TV's *The National*, donating thousands of dollars' worth of volunteer labour to seniors. In the meantime, my phone was ringing off the hook. I wasn't surprised; Canadians have been known to be very generous with charitable donations.

COURTESY, CONSTRUCTION VOLUNTEERS CANADA

After much persistence, I connected with a large emergency coordination centre in Quebec. I was provided with a list of communities seeking assistance. I chose St-Valentin, Quebec, because I am a romantic by nature. There was a lovers festival in the offing and the roads needed to be cleared of debris or the festival would be cancelled.

I was convinced that with the help of God I could accomplish the impossible. I drew on my inner strength, and all the teachings of the Bible. I tried hard to see God's image in the faces of strangers; I walked with them into dangerous situations and held their hands. I knew God was holding my right hand and I wasn't afraid; with the left hand I held the victim's hand.

The Tree Specialists, Inc., of Oakville, Ontario, the third group of tree experts, accompanied me into St-Valentin, Quebec. I didn't have construction boots and I was sliding on the ice, so a kind arborist loaned me a second-hand pair of steel-toed boots, one size too big for me. I stuffed them with paper to make them fit. Our group stayed in Quebec for one month. The language barrier was not a problem after all. Quebecers tried their best to make us feel comfortable and translated jokes for our benefit. They even described in detail how maple sugar is made and unfortunately, I ate too many sugar pies and gained 15 pounds. I was so heartsick about leaving these kind and generous people that I hitched a ride on a sausage delivery truck and travelled to Montreal to seek additional volunteer tradesmen. I told them the smaller communities were suffering greatly and I watched in awe and disbelief as the donated trucks and volunteer tradesmen from Montreal arrived in St-Valentin, just before we returned to Toronto.

Some people have referred to me as a hero since I began coordinating construction crews for disaster relief, but I have always felt the true heroes are the victims who rarely complain and who always put other people ahead of themselves. They say to me, "please help my neighbour," which brings tears to my eyes.

I thought that as I grew with the charity I founded, Construction Volunteers Canada, I'd stop crying and learn control and professionalism. I have never stopped crying and sometimes the victims console me. I hear and see horrific things. Our charity has mobilized after disasters such as the Ice Storm, floods, avalanches, and tornadoes in Ontario, Quebec, and Alberta.

COURTESY, CONSTRUCTION VOLUNTEERS CANADA

Disasters — demonstrating the raw power of nature — can be breathtaking, almost majestic, but they are also frightening, often life-threatening. Volunteers ignore the risks to themselves, expressing benevolence to their fellow human beings.

Unsung Heroes, a labour of love, tells the stories of Canadians helping Canadians in the face of natural disasters. More than 2,000 participants submitted their stories for this book; in fact, we received enough material for two books. We received submissions from adults and youth, but it is the young people who have been particularly excited about the project. I've included as many submissions as possible; my apologies to those whose submissions did not make it into this book. I would like to acknowledge the thousands of extraordinary Canadians who are not mentioned in this book who gave freely of their time following natural disasters for the love of our country and for their love of humankind. A special thank you to the churches, whose clergy and parishioners provide support in so many ways.

A portion of royalties from this book will be allocated to the communities represented by youth primarily for the emergency needs of youth following natural disasters. Children and teenagers reached beyond their youthful years to describe the intensity of the disasters. We encourage young people to volunteer and become more active in their communities. We believe that other people will be inspired by these good Samaritans.

My work with Construction Volunteers Canada has affected my life dramatically. I listen more intently to the news, particularly disaster coverage. I fund this charity out of my own pocket; it has been very difficult. One-hundred percent of the donations we receive are allocated to the victims' needs. But though it has been difficult financially, I press on because I am determined to continue God's work.

Nancy Loewen
President and Founder, Construction Volunteers Canada/
Bénévoles Canadiens du Bâtiment

CHAPTER 1

The Great Ice Storm of 1998

DND CANADA

A typical sight during the Ice Storm.

FOR THE RECORD

- 35 people died from storm-related causes
- 100 mm of freezing rain fell
- 120,000 km of power lines and telephone cables were downed
- 130 high-voltage transmission towers collapsed
- 30,000 wooden utility poles fell
- 54 communities in Eastern Ontario declared states of emergency
- $500-million in damage was accrued
- millions of trees were damaged or destroyed
- power was cut off to approximately 100,000 homes in eastern Ontario and 900,000 homes in Quebec
- 500,000 Ontarians were without electricity, some for more than three weeks
- 120,000 of Ontario Hydro's 165,000 customers in eastern Ontario were left without heat or light, many without phone service
- The Insurance Bureau of Canada received claims totalling more than $138 million by February 1998
- 16,000 military personnel were deployed

IT IS NOW REFERRED TO AS THE GREAT ICE STORM OF 1998, BUT AT THE TIME it was happening no one could gauge the severity or the extent of the damage that would be caused when 100 millimetres of freezing rain poured over parts of eastern Canada and the northeastern United States, icing everything in its path. Within days, more than a million households, businesses, stores, and schools had been plunged into darkness and extreme cold — frozen in their tracks. Environment Canada states that a storm of such drastic proportions occurs only once every few hundred years. The time had clearly arrived for this one.

DND CANADA

Anatomy of a Storm: The Ice Storm

Freezing rain is a common winter hazard in Canada. So how did the 1998 Ice Storm become the most expensive storm in Canadian history, crippling much of eastern Ontario and Quebec?

In an average year, Ottawa and Montreal receive between 45 and 65 hours of freezing rain, spread out over the entire winter. During the Ice Storm, they were dealt more than 80 hours worth in five days. A "bad" ice storm may mean 30 to 40 millimetres of freezing rain; the 1998 Ice Storm rained down 100 millimetres — that's a 4-inch casing of ice on everything. And because the Ice Storm struck all along the St. Lawrence valley, at its peak reaching from Muskoka to the Fundy coast and south into New York and New England, the extent of the damage and the number of people in need were dramatically higher than in any storm in Canadian history.

How did this happen? As with most natural disasters, it was the meeting of several coincidental weather patterns that led to this record-breaking storm. Three successive warm humid fronts from the Gulf of Mexico were moving up the East Coast, possibly as a result of El Niño. In many of the northeastern states, they brought heavy rains and flooding. Upon reaching the St. Lawrence River, they moved over a cold front that had settled in the valley. The cold front was only a few degrees below zero, creating the perfect conditions for freezing rain.

Freezing rain occurs when a warm front (above freezing) passes over a cold front (below freezing). Precipitation, which either comes from the warm front itself as rain or is melted to rain while falling through the warm front, is supercooled as it falls through the cold front beneath. This means that the water temperature of the raindrop actually drops below zero, although the rain remains in liquid form. Upon striking anything cold, whether road, tree, car, or house, the rain instantly freezes, forming a slick coating of ice on whatever it touches.

Due to surrounding wind patterns, the unusually wet weather responsible for the Ice Storm was trapped for five days over the same region, making a bad storm into a disaster. The sheer weight of the ice tore apart millions of trees and collapsed 130 transmission towers, 30,000 utility poles, and 120,000 kilometres of power and telephone cables. The ice covered roads, train tracks, and airport runways, making transportation virtually impossible for days or, in most rural areas, weeks. And because the Ice Storm hit such a highly populated area, it left more than 4 million people to freeze in the dark for days, with temperatures dropping below −15°C. An estimated 70,000 people living in rural areas were still without power three weeks after the storm. Any building with a generator became a shelter, and thousands sought refuge in these places. Farmers were especially hard hit: With no way to provide heat for their livestock, they were helpless as thousands of their animals died. At least 25 people also died, some from the cold, and others when the fires they were using to keep warm burned out of control, claiming houses and lives.

The Air Force Flies to the Rescue

When the Ice Storm hit eastern Canada in the winter of 1998, millions of Canadians were plunged into cold and darkness. The Air Force helped hydro crews restore heat and light to beleaguered communities, moved electrical generators, cleared dangerous debris, helped people get to shelters, and transported those who needed medical assistance.

Twenty-nine CH-146 Griffon helicopters were deployed throughout Ontario, Quebec, and New Brunswick. In all, 30 Air Force units lent their support, with flying squadrons, airfield engineering units, and security forces each playing a vital role. Their missions included the establishment of an "air bridge" for supplies and more than 100 airlifts in and out of areas crippled by the storm.

The Griffon helicopter crews also flew reconnaissance missions for Hydro-Québec. As well as being the eyes in the sky for those coordinating relief and repair operations, the helicopters ferried equipment, supplies, and people to where they were most needed. Crews also flew over affected power lines, carefully knocking off ice accumulations to prevent further damage and power outages. On the ground, Air Force personnel cooked meals, repaired generators, and chopped wood. Across Canada, Air Force Wings collected and shipped supplies and generators to the region. In all, more than 16,000 military personnel participated in Operation Recuperation.

— Kristina Davis, *Maple Leaf*

The Aurora aircraft, normally used for maritime coastal and anti-submarine patrol, used sophisticated surveillance and communications equipment to relay information to ground-based personnel. — DND Canada

The Ice Storm wasn't just a storm that covered roads with snow and left rooftops icy, it was a disaster. It was as though nature was on a rampage. Ontario's volunteer spirit and generosity reached out to helpless victims. The Salvation Army and other charities donated funds and goods. Our nation of care and goodwill overcame a natural catastrophe.

Nancy Jebran
Ascension of Our Lord Secondary School
Mississauga, Ontario

COURTESY DIANE AND YVON FOURNIER, ST-VALENTIN, QUEBEC

DND CANADA

A soldier chainsaws fallen tree branches for easier clean-up.

COURTESY, CONSTRUCTION VOLUNTEERS CANADA

While Hugh Gallaugher was at his pharmacy, his son, Matthew, had to hold a flashlight for him so that he could see to type labels and count tablets. After 4 p.m., it was too dark to do anything at all. A lot of people came into the pharmacy for batteries and soon he was sold out. He also supplied baby formula to a number of families. His biggest problem was that none of the computer systems were working: He could not get information from the customers' files. Dad hopes that it will be another 50 years before an ice storm hits again.

Gina Gallaugher
St. Joseph Catholic School
Prescott, Ontario

I have volunteered for many things in my life including donating to the Salvation Army, which opens shelters and supplies emergency kits. I think volunteering is important because it takes only a little bit of your time to make a large impact on someone else's life.

Jonathan Ehmann
École W.S. Hawrylak School
Regina, Saskatchewan

A volunteer pruning trees in St-Valentin. This type of work was difficult and dangerous. Workers could easily slip on the ice and fall out of a tree.

Like others across Canada, I was mesmerized by the drama unfolding in eastern Ontario, Quebec, and New Brunswick, and by the visual and audible toll it was taking. One of the sounds etched in the minds of many people who lived through the storm is of the trees cracking, snapping apart, and thundering to the ground, under the weight of the ice coating their branches.

The Canadian Red Cross

As the frequency and magnitude of disasters increase, so must the capacity of the Canadian Red Cross to respond. Canadian Red Cross assistance can range from the provision of food and shelter to assisting evacuees in returning to their homes. Most of that help is dispensed through a network of more than 6,000 volunteers specifically trained to respond to disasters of all sizes at a moment's notice.

— The Canadian Red Cross

COURTESY, CONSTRUCTION VOLUNTEERS CANADA

With a volunteer from The Tree Specialists, Inc., surveying damage in Mt. Royal Park, Montreal, Quebec.

Even with the problems at home in Spencerville, I still found time to help people, and that made me feel good.

Joe Hendriks, as told to Eric Hendriks
St. Joseph Catholic School • Prescott, Ontario

One thing to remember in times of disaster is the emotions we experience — worry, sadness, nervousness, and fear are all normal emotions during and after such a traumatic crisis. It takes time to create an environment that provides a true sense of safety and security.

— Kathy Putnam,
Brockville Psychiatric Hospital,
Brockville, Ontario, as told to Julie Putnam,
St. Joseph School • Prescott, Ontario

Heroes of the Storm Fight the Cold War

In January 1998, Canadian Forces soldiers served on the front lines of the worst ice storm of the century. Ice accumulated from a series of storms, wreaking devastation in Ottawa, Montreal, the Maritimes, and everywhere in between. The devastation was so great that the storm was described as the worst and most expensive natural disaster in Canadian history.

The call for military help came from Quebec on January 9. The same request came from Ontario the next day. The Canadian Forces responded immediately with Operation

DND CANADA

Griffon helicopter crews flew missions to support Hydro-Québec, Ontario Hydro, and provincial emergency officials. The crews evacuated people stranded in their homes and carried the sick to medical facilities. Here, Prime Minister Jean Chrétien (inside helicopter) and TV crews are delivered into the devastation.

DND CANADA

DND CANADA

Recuperation. Close to 16,000 Regular and Reserve personnel were deployed from across Canada. More than 10,000 were sent to the Montreal area. Some 4,500 were deployed to the Ottawa area and 393 deployed to St. John, New Brunswick.

Thousands more military and civilian personnel worked long hours behind the scenes to support those deployed on the front lines. The result: the greatest Canadian humanitarian operation by the military in post-war Canadian history.

The soldiers cleared roads, cut firewood, trimmed trees, pumped water from flooded basements, carried the sick to hospital, worked with power crews to restore electrical power and generally ensure the safety of local citizens.

Throughout the Montreal region, the area hardest hit by the ice storm, people streamed out of their candlelit homes to greet the troops, offering coffee, sandwiches, and cakes. Soldiers and emergency officials went door to door checking on house-bound people, who after a week without heat, hot water, or electricity were facing increased risks as temperatures dropped to –20°C. By January 13, soldiers and 100 military police officers provided unarmed patrols of neighbourhoods, and accompanied police forces in the most devastated areas in and around Montreal.

Eight field kitchens were set up in Quebec. These mobile kitchens were equipped to feed up to 1,000 people per meal. The military also provided aircraft and crews to move essential items across Canada to areas devastated by the storms. At least 8,000 camp cots, as well as large quantities of air mattresses, sleeping bags, generators, and other equipment were distributed by the Canadian Forces.

— Anne Boys, *Maple Leaf*

DND CANADA

The army helps out in Montreal during the Ice Storm.

The Cot Man

When the soldiers from northern Ontario arrived in Embrun, they found the villagers sleeping on the floor of their local shelter. So they collected their own cots and sent 20-year-old Private Stephane Audet back with the load.

He delivered 31 cots to the village east of Ottawa and found the relief shelter in chaos. No real organization existed. Stephane soon earned the name "Cot Man" and provided the leadership the centre desperately needed during the Ice Storm of 1998.

At first, Stephane was overwhelmed by the disorder around him as he helped people, but within two hours he had the place under control.

He quickly guided the townspeople to help themselves. He set up work crews to start cleaning and established a first-aid point. He set up and organized a message board where information for services and vital phone numbers could be located quickly and easily. "It was amazing what he did," said Larry Crossley of Embrun.

There were tears in the eyes of local residents a couple of days later when Stephane prepared to leave. They wanted their Private Audet back.

— Jon O'Connor, *Garrison*

At the fire hall, the men were split into teams. Their first priority was the old-age homes and shelters where the generators needed to be fueled and kept running. When asked what he remembered most, Paul Arcand, a volunteer firefighter in Prescott, Ontario, recalled how everyone worked well together to get the job done. "No one concerned themselves with stress or money, they just concentrated on the task at hand." Paul reported that they stood guard at all entrances to the town and patrolled streets. Paul cut branches and helped with the hydro hook-ups from the ground.

Paul Arcand, as told to Kelly J. Cole-Arcand
St. Joseph Catholic School
Prescott, Ontario

People helped each other, and I shared my generator with my neighbours. My biggest problem was not getting enough sleep.

Adrian Wynands, as told to Ryan Wynands
St. Joseph Catholic School
Prescott, Ontario

On the radio we had heard about a family with two children whose house had burned to the ground. We packed up some clothes, some books, and some toys for the family.

Patty Arcand, as told to Jessica Arcand
St. Joseph Catholic School
Prescott, Ontario

DND CANADA

"You'd lie in bed at night and hear these terrific crashes and you'd wonder which tree had just ripped apart in your backyard," recalls Natalie Harris of the Kinette Club of Charlotte Fundy, New Brunswick. "When you're losing 10 or 12 trees that are each 50 or 60 years old, it's a big loss."

Admittedly, trees are the furthest thing from peoples' minds at a time like this, but it was apparent to me, watching all this on my television in Toronto, that the falling trees were not only severely damaged, they were a frightening risk to people and property. The falling trees and branches so littered streets and fields that hydro crews found it impossible to reach power lines and attempt to restore electricity. A young mother and child were sobbing in a Quebec shelter because they couldn't return to their home.

That's when I called Al Miley, an arborist in Toronto. Al would become one of countless unsung heroes of the Ice Storm. "Are you busy?" I asked Al on the phone that early January day, knowing full well that a man with a tree-cutting business couldn't be doing too much at that time of year.

The people who survived the Ice Storm were depressed for many months afterwards. Many wondered if their communities would ever be the same. If I had lived in the area during the Ice Storm, I would want to make sure I was prepared for an ice storm or any other natural disaster in the future.

Stephanie Lamoureaux
Canadian Martyrs Catholic School
Oshawa, Ontario

An unknown record was lived upon thousands of freezing faces. We fought and showed our strength, leaving behind our fears.

— Kim Vigneault
Richmond Regional High School
Richmond, Quebec

COURTESY DND

On the first day of the Ice Storm in Gatineau we were so happy to visit our Grandpa. We were surprised that grandpa had electricity. We spent most of our day outside having a snowball fight, making a snowman, and sliding.

Lisa Laframboise
Hadley Junior High School
Hull, Quebec

The Ice Storm brought out the best in most people. One man from my mom's work took a week off, and every day that week he took his generator house to house, an hour for every house he went to. He helped out 10 to 12 homes each day until the power in his area was back on. If this happened again, I'd collect food for emergency shelters.

Michael David
Blessed Kateri Tekakwitha School
Orleans, Ontario

The Masons Take on the Challenge of the Storm

A small Masonic lodge in the Ottawa Valley grouped together to help out their community in the face of the storm of the century. But it wasn't easy.

Birches by the roadside bent in arcs, molding with the ground. They formed tunnels of ice and bark. White scars of shattered wood scarred every woodlot, most of the fractures 20 feet above ground level, and not a leaf on the tree. It looked as if a malevolent monster had judo-chopped the forest, shattering some trees, toppling others, and ignoring those that would bend. It seemed like an aftermath of an artillery barrage in World War I.

Lone trees in the center of a pasture were quartered and on the ground, like huge bananas, peeled and dropped. And the same ice coating took down wooden hydro poles and the lines they supported.

Senior Deacon Roger Belanger recalls his slow introduction to the disaster. "I went to the church to shave," he recalls. "We were passing Marty Albright that night and the power had gone out at my place. It was still patchy around town. Eventually it went out everywhere, then it was like the 1930s with everyone burning oil lamps."

It didn't take long for the networking to start, and the first need was for power generators, from friends of Roger's cousin in Windsor. "I asked him on the phone how much the generator would cost, and again when he delivered it, but he said he didn't know. When he finally did name the price, I tried to give him the money, and he said, 'Keep it. I'll just lose it. See me later.'"

The next task: how could 15,000 pounds of fresh potatoes be distributed? The City of Burlington, paired with Vankleek Hill, trucked in 150 hundred-pound sacks of potatoes. The same truck carried five cords of split wood, blankets, clothing, cartons of batteries — cells for flashlights. CAFÉ (Community Assistance Fund Enterprise) had the expertise and volunteers to serve and take in the entire community.

Soldiers and volunteer firemen made the rounds of all the houses, paying special attention to the elderly. But the reception was not always friendly. Two octogenarians and their

42-year-old son posted a sign on their gate: "We are three adults and we are fine. Canadian Army leave us alone."

The crew did more than ask questions. They lugged the portable generators from house to house. Those with oil furnaces were given three hours of "juice" to fire up their furnaces and heat their houses, maybe even to get enough hot water for a shower. Then, on to the next cold house, while the last one started to chill down until its next transfusion of electrons.

DND CANADA

Acts of kindness were practical and often a surprise. The Mayor of Southampton phoned and was told that, indeed, generators were needed. He arrived late at night with nine of them in his trailer, several chainsaws, and a cheque for $5,000 from the town. The "Stones" event at SkyDome in Toronto was scrubbed, so two tractor trailers loaded with food, generators, refrigeration, propane, stoves, and chefs made the six-hour trek to Vankleek Hill.

— Ted Morris and William T. Anderson

DND CANADA

My family and I were some of the lucky ones because we lost our power for about 10 seconds, while others lost it for days, weeks. The military was a great help by providing shelter and food. There were people who gave up their privacy, food, and homes just so another family, who they might not even have known, could feel comfortable, safe, and at home. These people really made a difference. If it wasn't for the fact that we all helped each other out, it would have been worse and because of that, a terrible disaster wasn't as terrible as it could have been.

Andrew Mott

Blessed Kateri Tekakwitha School

Orleans, Ontario

COURTESY, CONSTRUCTION VOLUNTEERS CANADA

Feeding horses on a farm in the St-Valentin area. This particular horse was hurt in the Ice Storm when a chunk of ice fell off a building onto its back.

The Unofficial Mayor of Vernon

Shivering in a small back room of a building — the only room heated in the emergency shelter — were the citizens of the village of Vernon, Ontario.

Like many people in Ontario, Quebec, and the Maritimes, the people had to leave their homes during the Ice Storm of 1998. The village of Vernon lost its power late on a Monday evening. Five days later Corporal Sean Scullion, a soldier with the Royal Canadian Dragoons in Petawawa, Ontario, arrived at the Vernon Recreation Centre.

"We had nothing until he showed up," said Erin Franed. His wife Mary agreed: "People here were sure happy to see the army!"

The two Baker brothers, both in their eighties, had been sleeping in two chairs for the past four days. When Sean saw them, he knew he had to do something. He got on his radio and didn't quit until he got what the villagers needed.

The first thing they needed was heat. Soon an Air Canada de-icing machine was parked outside the recreation centre. Like a monstrous hair dryer, it pumped hot air through a big hose into the building.

Then Sean organized all the people anxious to volunteer themselves and their resources. He kept the kids entertained, painting their faces with a camouflage stick.

"We've made him the unofficial mayor," laughed Mr Franed. "I wish Sean were our neighbour!" added his seven-year-old son.

After being cooped up together for more than a week as they waited for the lights to come back on, Sean and the villagers became close friends.

"I love this place," Sean said. "All I want to do, when all this is over, is to be able to come back and relax."

— Captain Bob Kennedy,
Canadian Forces

It's all so surreal, like one of those dreams where you're the only person left in the world. But everyone's inside, sealed in by a layer of ice. The silence is broken now and then by sounds that bring me back to this frozen reality: a transformer explodes, sending blue and purple light into the sky, or a branch snaps, finally exhausted by its icy burden. This will all be over soon, I know. The lights will go on and the ice will melt away and we'll be free again. But now our lives stand still, almost as if time is frozen, too.

Jessica Howarth
Lindsay Place High School
Pointe-Claire, Quebec

DND CANADA

COURTESY, CONSTRUCTION VOLUNTEERS CANADA

A volunteer takes a break from his efforts.

Perth Helps Out Its Own

By Thursday, January 7, it was evident that our worst fears would be realized. More than 65 millimetres of freezing rain had fallen to this point, coating everything with a thick layer of ice, and there was no let-up in sight. On Monday, the rain that had fallen had looked like a disaster area. The weight of the ice had broken the tops off trees, roads were closed, hydro lines had broken and fallen to the ground, and hydro poles had been snapped off at ground level. Entire portions of the area were left in darkness. The Mayor of Perth, for the first time in our history, declared a state of emergency. The shelter at the Perth Civitan hall would become a necessity for many people.

Members of the club were called to the Perth Civitan Hall and Civitans took the initiative of providing shelter for the residents of their community. We collected cots and mattresses from the Salvation Army, members of the community, and the Town of Perth Emergency Committee. The police and fire departments were made aware that Civitans were able to provide food and lodging at their hall. Donations of food poured in from individuals and businesses. The military arrived with a generator. During the 12 days the shelter was open, approximately 5,000 meals were served.

We first cared for two busloads of seniors who were without heat and hydro. They were brought to the hall and treated to a hot meal of soup and sandwiches on Thursday evening. The reality of the storm had not as yet set in and these people returned to their seniors' residence, which was still without heat and hydro.

— The Perth Civitan Club

"Yes, I am busy," he chuckled. "I'm busy watching soap operas."

We talked about the storm, and I asked if he would volunteer his time, skills, and equipment in Goulburn, a township southwest of Ottawa. Later on I would deploy him and his volunteer crews to Orangeville, Ontario, Oka and St. Placide, Quebec.

Al was amazing. He didn't flinch; he jumped right in to help. He and his younger brother, Brian, also an arborist, rounded up a 15-man crew — all of them experienced tree climbers from the Mississauga First Nations reserve near Blind River, Ontario. They packed their trucks and wood chippers and headed to Goulburn. In the meantime, I called several other arborists seeking volunteer crews and donations of wood chippers. I made an appeal through the media and was overwhelmed by the positive response.

When Al Miley and the crews got there, the scene was worse than they expected in some ways, and not as bad in others. The ice was thick on the power lines — as thick as six inches in some places — but the good news was that it was melting off the tree branches.

"We had to use special precautions because there was so much debris," said Al. "It took a long time to reach some of those trees. Our job was to simply prune them, but in many cases the main sections of the trees had torn away, so we had to rebalance the tree both visually and structurally."

Al's crew pruned about 400 trees. They provided a month of free labour, which amounted to thousands of dollars.

"It was the first time I had volunteered for something," said Al. "I'm healthy, I can contribute. I also felt I had to do it. When I was in the midst of it, I realized how enormous it was, and why so many people were needed."

My list of commitments isn't the longest, but I put my heart into them all. My class, along with the help of the kindergarten class, planted 35 to 40 saplings. If Canada experiences another ice storm, there could be even fewer trees in our wonderful country.

Stefan Litalien

École W.S. Hawrylak School • Regina, Saskatchewan

Hydro-Québec Helps Out

The Ice Storm will remain forever etched in the memories of Hydro-Québec. It was a time of hardship overcome through sheer will and commitment.

No electricity, no telephone, no water, no husband or wife, no mother or father. That was the situation faced by many spouses and children of Hydro-Québec employees. They never questioned the fact that the employee had to work late and might not even come home for several nights. It was just accepted, and that acceptance was vital, though some employees still experienced difficult moments: a father trying to console his tearful little girl over the telephone, a mother worrying about leaving her young teenagers alone to deal with the wood stove, families forced to split up and stay with relatives. But they made it through the dark nights and cold days. To all those families, including mine, of course, a big thank you!

— André Caillé, President and CEO
Hydro-Québec

Toronto Fire Crews Help Out

Tasks were assigned by the Emergency Operations Centre. The people of Kingston helped my crew as much as we helped them. There was so much devastation that many areas looked like a war zone. Branches and wires were everywhere. I can still hear the loud crackle of branches and chunks of ice as our Emergency Support unit moved slowly along the residential streets in ruin. When we thought we could go no farther, people rushed out of their homes towards us with long boards. They positioned themselves on either side of the truck and, using the boards, pushed the wires up over the vehicle and waved us through. I gained so much more than I gave. It was a privilege to serve.

— Ray Easby,
City of Toronto Fire Department

It was a pervasive sentiment: The Ice Storm attracted all sorts of volunteers. I deployed volunteer labourers from Toronto into Mt. Royal Park, Montreal, and volunteer tree crews into St-Valentin, Oka, and St-Placide, Quebec and Goulbourn and Orangeville, Ontario.

Among the most visible of the volunteers were members of Canada's Air Force. They cooked meals, repaired generators, chopped wood, and looked in on people to see if they needed help. One couple who benefited from this assistance was Diane and Keith Forgie, who operate the Papanack Park Zoo near Wendover, Ontario. The zoo houses a range of exotic animals — timber wolves, cougars, Arctic foxes, baboons, and lions. The storm knocked out the zoo's power and phone for six days.

For the Forgies, the 427 Squadron from Canadian Forces Base Petawawa provided a lifeline: Military personnel would regularly check in on them, knowing the couple could not leave their animals unattended.

DND CANADA

While travelling to Montreal, I was struck by the aftermath of the 1998 Ice Storm. I observed with sadness the damage to the trees bordering the highway. The storm brought out the goodness of people. In the absence of electricity, some families were forced to heat their homes with fireplaces that were not designed to be burning on a continual basis. As a result, some houses were destroyed by fire. I personally believe this storm was a test of our faith and a test to see how we would help the people around us in times of need. The efforts of many communities suggests that we passed with flying colours.

Erika Fisher
St. Patrick's Intermediate School
Ottawa, Ontario

Mareth, who will eventually weigh about 650 lbs., rests in the arms of an Air Force officer.

My stepfather is in the Canadian Forces. At CFB Borden, everything didn't turn to ice, but everyone's life was turned upside down because the people from the base were sent to help the people in Quebec and eastern Ontario. Both moms and dads in some families left to help, and their children stayed with babysitters for two weeks and longer. Our parents drove in convoys to the unknown in treacherous road conditions. When they got to different towns they set up their cots in gymnasiums, shelters, and schools. They helped people clear trees, give rides, and distribute food, wood, and other supplies. They looked for people who might be stranded. And they hoped that if their family was ever in this kind of distress that someone from far away would help them, too.

Aaron Tilley
Prince of Peace Catholic School
Borden, Ontario

Helping Hands Across an Icy Quebec

DND CANADA

Thousands of soldiers pulled on their winter clothes, said goodbye to their families, and spread out across Quebec to help people dig out, warm up, and recover from the grips of the Ice Storm in 1998.

"Heroes? They're all heroes," said Captain Jean-Marc Lanthier, operations officer with 12 Armoured Regiment, based at Valcartier. "All those soldiers who went out and cut firewood for the population until their hands were blistered, then walked 15 kilometres back to Acton Vale in their mukluks — they're all heroes."

The soldiers worked in an area that measured more than 1,600 square kilometres. They distributed firewood, repaired almost 100 generators, provided security and medical assistance. There was only a minor hitch: The soldiers had to manage with cell phones because their communications system was in their vehicles, which they didn't bring to the clean-up operation.

In another part of Quebec, Private Sherry McGill didn't have any second thoughts about joining the army even as she worked in an open field, exposed to icy winds, near the village of Sainte-Sabine. As she helped comrades recover pieces of the downed power lines, other soldiers from 2 Troop and 1 Combat Engineer Regiment were digging the dead power lines out of deep ice with pickaxes.

Corporal Wayne Parks of 1 Princess Patricia's Canadian Light Infantry was conducting his patrol at a shelter for storm victims in St-Jean-sur-Richelieu in the early morning when he heard a woman call for help. He rushed to find a nurse trying to help an elderly woman, her lips blue. She did not appear to be breathing; Wayne couldn't locate a heartbeat. The young corporal checked her pupils and on his second attempt, her eyes finally flickered with signs of life. He moved swiftly to resuscitate her; nurses at the shelter said his actions saved the woman's life. Wayne — a reluctant hero — insisted that it was simply his army training. "I guess I just helped her out a little bit."

The grade of the small mountain was almost straight up and a platoon of Van Doos (the legendary Royal 22nd Regiment) was clearing a path through broken trees to a communications tower at the summit. It was tough, dangerous work, but Hydro-Québec needed the communications tower to help restore power in the region.

"Hydro-Québec asked them to do this because no one else could do it," said Major Daniel Massé, whose soldiers of B Company, 2 Battallion, Royal 22nd Regiment took on similar tasks throughout Operation Recuperation.

Major Benoit Proulx served as deputy commander, 35 Brigade, in the eastern half of Quebec. He spoke with obvious pride of the Reservists called up from Shawinigan, Rimouski, Lévis, Matane, and other cities and towns of eastern Quebec.

— Paul Mooney, *Maple Leaf*

My aunt lived in Ottawa when the terrible ice storm hit in 1998. She had no power for at least two or three weeks. She had a baby that was just a year old. They had to wear lots of warm clothes because they had no heat. There was no electricity. They had lots of candles so it was not as dark as it would be without them. They also had lots of blankets for when it got cold. This storm has changed my aunt's life.

Keirsten Gysbertsen
Fairview Heights Elementary School
Halifax, Nova Scotia

When the ice storm struck Gatineau, I was so incredibly happy that I didn't think of the danger that might follow, or of the homeless people with nowhere to go. All that I thought about was my nice, warm bed and getting a few more hours of some nice relaxing shut-eye. Two weeks later, my aunt and two annoying cousins came to stay at my house. It was horrible — I was kicked out of my nice comfy bed and stuck on the old lumpy couch. I had to listen to country music, and I did not get to watch any of my television shows between the power going out and the eight people inside my house. A few days later, I heard on the news that an elderly lady had died in her home because she had no heat. I started to think about my aunt and how that could have been her. She was in the exact same situation before she and my cousins came to stay with me and my family. So then I looked back and realized that, with everything that had happened, it was okay because I knew none of them were in any danger as long as they stayed with us.

Tiffany Martin
Hadley Junior High School
Hull, Quebec

The Kinsmen & Kinette Clubs of Canada Provide Hope

Along with promises of government aid came the deployment of 14,000 troops to help with clean-up, evacuation, and security. Offers of monetary and hands-on assistance came from several organizations, including Kinsmen & Kinette Clubs of Canada.

"I really believed Kin could play a role because of how we can mobilize people," said Carol Bowie of the Kinette Club of Brockville, Ontario, explaining why she launched the "Operation Kin Thaw" relief effort.

With $10,000 from Kin's National Disaster Fund already committed to the cause, Bowie put the call out to members across the country that more help was needed. Soon, a substantial supplement of more than $23,000 was raised.

Kinsmen and Kinettes were not content to help by fundraising alone, however. "We probably had about 85 percent of our local club members helping out at the shelters," said Bowie. "We were serving either one or two meals a day. I think we fed about 4,500 people at the busiest meal we had."

In Châteauguay and Montreal, members assisted at the food banks and soup kitchens, while, in two New Brunswick communities, funds were collected to replace 45 lost trees and to erect monuments to remind residents of the tremendous goodwill that resulted from the storm.

In Stoney Creek and Hamilton, Ontario members too distant to get involved in disaster site activities helped send several tractor-trailer loads of desperately needed supplies to hard-hit areas. "And this kind of generosity was being repeated in community after community," said Bowie. "I was amazed to see and hear about all the work people were willing to do. It was just so uplifting."

— Joseph Distel,
Kinsmen & Kinette Clubs of Canada

By looking out my window I could see how beautiful the ice made the trees look, especially when the sun made the ice glisten. My father, however, was aware of the damage this would cause the trees. I remember him taking my brother outside with hockey sticks and tapping at the ice on the branches. Many barns collapsed under the weight of the ice. Cows from dairy farms could not be milked. Cows developed pneumonia. Many stores donated generators to farms. Milk processing plants were shut down and more than 10 million gallons of milk had to be dumped.

Lisa Sarazin,
Blessed Kateri Tekakwitha School
Orleans, Ontario

Despite the risks of bad roads and falling ice, many people braved the elements to make life bearable for others. The Ice Storm of 1998 showed us all what Canadians are really made of — strength, endurance, and community spirit.

Sylvia Lima
St. Patrick's Intermediate School
Ottawa, Ontario

As a show of gratitude, Mr. Forgie allowed the squadron to adopt (in name only) a rare white lion, which they called Mareth. Lions are a tradition for the squadron: In 1942, the helicopter unit got its name, The Fighting Lions, when MGM Studios, famous for its roaring lion, adopted the squadron. The following year, Sir Winston Churchill presented the unit with a lion named Mareth.

COURTESY RCMP

Four members of the RCMP and one member of the Canadian Forces performed Dixieland music for Ice Storm victims around the Montreal area.

The same vigilance shown by the Forces was demonstrated by police officers, many of whom were storm victims themselves. The Ontario Provincial Police, armed with flashlights, checked empty businesses on darkened streets and patrolled roads and highways for stranded motorists. The Royal Canadian Mounted Police patrolled rural and urban areas, supplied homes with heat, hot water, and some light, started furnaces with the help of a generator in Cornwall and on the Akwesasne reserve, handled distress calls, cleared fallen trees and branches, removed ice from walkways and roofs, prepared and delivered meals, and ran garbage detail. They also provided the use of a helicopter, vehicles,

COURTESY, CONSTRUCTION VOLUNTEERS CANADA

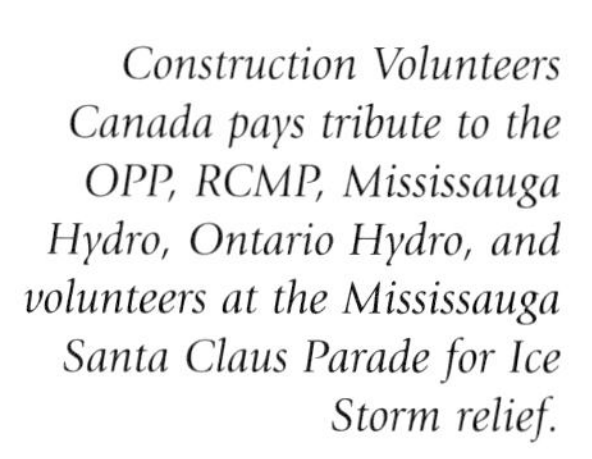

Construction Volunteers Canada pays tribute to the OPP, RCMP, Mississauga Hydro, Ontario Hydro, and volunteers at the Mississauga Santa Claus Parade for Ice Storm relief.

How the Y Helped Out

I remember that the height of the blackouts began on Monday, January 5, because I moved out of my cold apartment the following day. I moved myself and my two cats into the daycare centre at the Women's Y that Tuesday. The building still had power and we continued to offer our regular services to parents. We also extended our services to many other families. The homes of some parents and staff members did not have power, and they had no one to take them in. We opened our doors to those that needed a warm, safe place to be in the evening.

Since the downtown core was still up and running at that point, we could offer warm meals and evening entertainment for our guests. One evening, we were given hockey tickets to go see a Canadiens game at the Molson Centre. Another evening we used the swimming pool at the Women's Y, and the final evening we watched movies and ate popcorn.

— Andria Mallozzi,
The Women's Y of Montreal

At the beginning, we worked non-stop, 24 hours a day. We communicated by telephone and two-way radio. The rain wouldn't quit. Power lines were down, and Ontario Hydro couldn't provide power. My family and I were fortunate during the storm. We camp in the summer, so we had some supplies and a wood stove.

Bill Lawrence, Prescott Fire Chief,
as told to Alex Hewson
St. Joseph Catholic School • Prescott, Ontario

Neighbours hauled generators donated by Hydro-Québec from house to house. Soldiers carried senior citizens from broken-down houses to protective havens. The YMCA opened its doors to all in need, making their equipment, services, and rooms available free of charge. There were donations of blankets and warm clothes, and many volunteers reached out to the needy. Not only was this a story of disaster, but testimony to remarkable friendship, strength, and courage.

Shawnakaye Vassel
Ascension of Our Lord Secondary School
Mississauga, Ontario

St. John Ambulance to the Rescue

As municipality after municipality declared a state of emergency, St. John Ambulance volunteers were already on their way to the affected areas, undeterred even by the loss of power and telephone service at both the national and Quebec headquarters. They brought much-needed generators, mobile first-aid units, a canteen, a command post, and even baby food.

When they arrived in the storm-ravaged area, volunteers were amazed at the reality of what they had seen on television. Huge hydro towers had crumpled under the weight of the ice; telephone poles lay snapped like kindling, while exhausted local residents worked all day just to find water and fuel.

In one heroic instance, a diabetic man, after a day alone in his cold home near Brockville, Ontario, finally received his crucial supply of insulin. Two St. John Ambulance volunteers drove eight hours from the other side of the province to help. They kept his insulin at the proper temperature, and eventually persuaded the man to go to a hospital, where he could get the care he needed.

After five tiring days spent supplying medicine, checking on people in their homes, and even peeling potatoes in shelters, volunteers from Tillsonburg, Ontario, said they'd have many good memories of the new friendships they formed. They look forward to returning for a visit in less stressful times.

— *St. John Canada Today* magazine

Looking Back on the Storm of the Century

RCMP employees made a remarkable contribution to easing the suffering of storm victims whose homes were without heat, electricity, telephones, and even water. Power was cut off to approximately 100,000 households in eastern Ontario and 900,000 households in Quebec. Members of "O" Division assisted elderly Kingston residents and patrolled affected areas. In Cornwall, Mounties were starting furnaces with a generator both around the town and on the Akwesasne reserve. "C" Division lent equipment and vehicles to the Montréal Urban Community Police for their relief efforts, and assigned officers in 17 police vehicles to provide help and a visible presence. They helped the Sûreté du Québec officers with door-to-door checks and evacuations of homes without power. Insp. Gary Clement of "A" Division distributed 85 generators to needy residents and farmers in the Metcalfe and Osgoode areas outside of Ottawa. In Kemptville, volunteer members helped prepare meals, run garbage details, and handle distress calls at the town's training centre. The Canadian Police College and the RCMP's Long Island Camp just south of Ottawa offered shelter for several days and nights.

COURTESY, CONSTRUCTION VOLUNTEERS CANADA

Presenting a plaque to RCMP officers for their efforts during the Ice Storm.

— Janice Burrows, RCMP.
Reprinted from the
RCMP Quarterly magazine with the permission of the
Royal Canadian Mounted Police

I was caught in a violent storm in Val des Monts, St. Pierre. My family and I stayed with a friend because he had a wood stove. They also had a generator, but the refrigerator wouldn't work so we put all the dairy products outside. After seven or eight weeks, we returned home.

Ricky Mesyjasz,
Hadley Junior High School
Hull, Quebec

It was cold and dark. There was no power. My dad called for a pizza and was told it would be there in two to three hours. It was white and icy outside. The tree branches were covered in ice. Everyone was inside wrapped in blankets. I remember sitting in my rocking chair listening to trees fall.

Ashley Smith,
Hadley Junior High School
Hull, Quebec

DND CANADA

generators, chainsaws, and other equipment. The Mounties even put together a Dixieland band and entertained storm-fatigued souls in several shelters. Many officers also took up collections for those hardest hit by the storm. One division raised $6,870; another collected enough money to pay for an order of groceries and supplies for Wakefield, Quebec.

Air reservists across Canada also lent a hand. Flying squadrons airlifted equipment, people, and supplies and assisted hydro workers by locating damaged power lines. On the ground, reservists cleared the mounds of fallen tree limbs, repaired generators, assisted hydro crews, and transported people to shelters and hospitals.

As Major Clifford Patterson recalls, "I went to the Cumberland firehall (just outside Ottawa) and asked what we as a community could do to help. Although I was not wearing my uniform, my neighbours and I had a small part in ensuring that the troops actively involved in the operation were fed and cared for."

Corporations, too, helped people and communities get back on their feet: Shell Canada donated more than 20,000 litres of fuel to enable

It was scary — it was like another Ice Age — but we beat it and survived. People were not prepared. They didn't have batteries or kerosene. I think if God had a purpose for this storm, it was to make us not look inwardly at ourselves, but rather to help people and bring people closer together.

Bruce Wylie of CFJR, Brockville,
as told to Keith Patterson
St. Joseph Catholic School
Prescott, Ontario

COURTESY, CONSTRUCTION VOLUNTEERS CANADA

A homeowner removing snow and ice from roof. The house is decorated for the annual St-Valentin Lovers Festival.

Ottawa's Ice Storm '98

In less than seven months of being open, our Nepean store had our first opportunity to experience the Home Depot culture in full force. On Tuesday, January 6, 1998 the Ottawa-Carleton area began to experience some freezing rain which slowly began to cover the city with a blanket of ice. By Thursday, January 8, a State of Emergency was called for the Ottawa area. Freezing rain continued knocking down trees, powerlines and hydro lines leaving thousands of residents without power or heat. One of our associates, Scott Kealey felt we could help our community so Scott and a co-worker, Louis Demarco went above and beyond the call of duty by organizing supplies and generators and bailing out flooded basements. Help was even extended to some of our own associates who did not have heat and power and whose basements were damaged extensively. Even our neighbouring Home Depot stores from the Toronto area caught the team depot spirit and without hesitation, brought their convoy of Ryder trucks, manpower and supplies, along with warmth, compassion and hope.

—Ivana Vlcek, Kanata Store

The Royal Canadian Legion Lends a Hand

The Legion, along with civic authorities and such organizations as the Salvation Army, was quick to react to the plight of the storm victims. Legions in the areas affected in both Ontario and Quebec, many of them also without light and power, hooked up generators, and provided hot meals and shelter space, paying for it all from their own

DND CANADA

resources. Dominion Command offered $25,000 in contingency funding for use as directed by the Ontario and Quebec commands. A $20,000 donation was made by the Ontario Command for the Canadian Red Cross.

As usual in a disaster situation, some businesses and individuals made a lasting impression on the long-suffering ice storm victims. One business, Amber's Café in Helvella, south of Ottawa, will never be forgotten by residents of this farming community. Sue Armstrong, who operates the business, was without power for 12 days but continued to keep the restaurant open and gave out hundreds of meals free to the storm victims in the community. "We all needed each other," said Armstrong. "I had just got in a shipment of bread before the storm. People in the community gave me food that would have spoiled in their refrigerators and freezers. These people in their cold and dark homes needed somewhere to come for a hot meal and companionship. I had a propane stove, grill, and pizza oven, and lots of candles for light." She even sent out food in care packages, delivered by the military troops, to stormbound residents who couldn't make it into her café. "The military men deserve the biggest pat on the shoulder ever," said Armstrong. "They really came through for us, and once they got there they didn't leave until the power was restored and the crisis was over."

— Ray Dick, *Legion Magazine*

COURTESY, CONSTRUCTION VOLUNTEERS CANADA

A volunteer from Al Miley and Associates, Orangeville, Ontario.

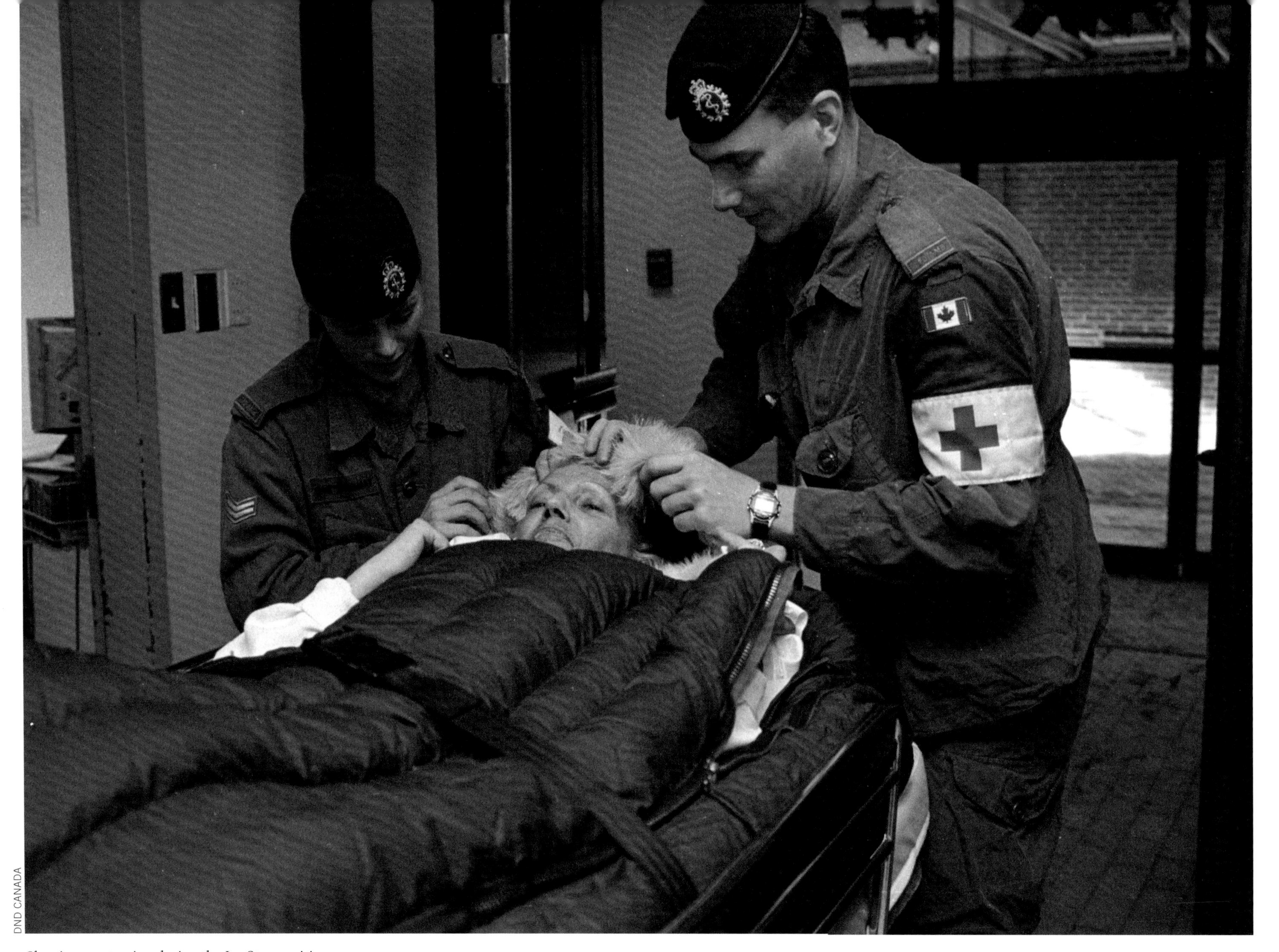

DND CANADA

Showing compassion during the Ice Storm crisis.

Captain Bill Nalepka and the Canadian Owners and Pilots Association to fly relief missions to St-Jean-sur-Richelieu, a city of 40,000 that was without power. The City of Toronto co-ordinated the delivery of supplies. GIFT, the grocery industry's charitable division, donated food. The Toronto Hotel Association provided bed linens and towels. Various hospitals and suppliers donated medical supplies. City of Toronto fire and police departments donated equipment. The City of Montreal's

COURTESY, CONSTRUCTION VOLUNTEERS CANADA

St-Valentin, Quebec, is twinned with Sakuto-Cho, Japan. The delegation travelled to Quebec to support Quebecers in their time of need.

Schools Chip In

Students at Mary Honeywell Elementary School raised $700 toward the Ice Storm Relief Fund effort by collecting loonies and toonies during the week following the return to school. Robert Hopkins Public School organized a disaster relief fund campaign entitled Every Penny Counts, and raised $210. Students also baked cookies and delivered them to local fire stations for distribution to those in need, and collected money by doing additional chores at home or in their neighbourhoods. Proceeds went to the Canadian Red Cross. Bell's Corners Public School held a change drive: Kindergarten to Grade 5 students raised $538.68 for the Canadian Red Cross. Forest Valley Elementary School donated $200, and Emily Carr Middle School donated $500 toward the Ice Storm Relief Fund. Students and staff of Agincourt Road Public School donated $419.17 to the Canadian Red Cross for victims of the Ice Storm. Some students who organized fundraising activities and contributed to the relief effort had also lived without electricity for some time.

— Hyacinth Haddad,
Communications and Information Services,
Ottawa-Carleton District School Board

My great-aunts and great-uncles lived together in one house, without electricity, running water, or telephones throughout the 16-day ordeal. January 10 was an important day — now two people a day could have a shower. Imagine being the other people who didn't. My family had to clean out their freezers and keep the food outside in large tubs with lids. That created another problem: the wild animals were hungry, too, because it was hard for them to get any food with the thick ice everywhere. The animals would break into people's food containers and eat all the food. One problem seemed to lead to many more. The RCMP were very good, coming to Loch Garry to check on people.

Alexandra McDonald
Blessed Kateri Tekakwitha School
Orleans, Ontario

Volunteer work is an important life process. If I had been in the Ice Storm, I would have read to the elderly.

Alicia Olson
École W.S. Hawrylak School
Regina, Saskatchewan

Each class had a container and collected money for the Ice Storm victims. We collected money for about two weeks. Everyone brought in their pennies. We worked hard and managed to raise $170, but we sent $200.

Kristy Macklaim
Huntsville Public School
Huntsville, Ontario

COURTESY, CONSTRUCTION VOLUNTEERS CANADA

With St-Valentin, Quebec, mayor René Trahan and his wife, Christine, in Yvon Landry's barn during the Ice Storm.

The Contribution of the Society of St. Vincent de Paul

The members of the Society of St. Vincent de Paul visited neighbouring villages and stopped in at shelter centres. In response to requests from authorities, the SSVP delivered fresh fruit and vegetables, blankets, and pillows to the shelter centres for almost two weeks. Vincentians were proud to help the members of a family whose home was completely destroyed by fire right in the middle of the Ice Storm. Immediately after the fire, we provided them with clothing, food, and replacement furniture. Our volunteers also helped in areas that were receiving little or no assistance. Although all those villages were located outside our territory and at distances as far away as the Quebec border, we were there.

The Vincentians collected $129,168.41 for relief efforts, which was sent on to the Quebec Provincial Council through our National Council. We are proud of all the assistance we were able to provide.

— *St. Vincent de Paul* magazine

If you didn't have a wood stove, it was nearly impossible to keep warm, and several people died of hypothermia. Others died from being hit by falling tree limbs and telephone poles. There were more than 25 deaths blamed on this storm. Volunteer firefighters drove around the countryside with generators to pump the water out of flooded basements. They also watered livestock for farmers. This storm brought out the best in people and showed how communities can pull together.

Shannon McKenzie and Stephanie Thompson
Prince Philip Public School
Niagara Falls, Ontario

Ice Storm 1998 — Provincial Operations Centre

Although it was miles away from the Ice Storm, there couldn't have been more action than at the Provincial Operations Centre (POC), located at Emergency Management Ontario in downtown Toronto.

Remember the scene of NASA's control room in the movie *Apollo 13*? That's how the POC appeared during the height of the storm — constant, round-the-clock activity, row upon row of computers, TV monitors placed strategically on the walls and maps marked to indicate communities that had declared emergencies.

Despite the crowded conditions, long hours, and constantly ringing telephones, employees were energized and coordinated efforts in an unprecedented way, says Dr. James Young, assistant deputy minister of the public safety division and official spokesperson for the province during the emergency.

— Excerpt from "Employees to the Rescue,"
TOPICAL newsletter, February 20, 1998.

COURTESY JACQUELINE AND YVON LANDRY, ST-VALENTIN, QUEBEC

For the first couple days of the storm, I stayed close to my family. We had to evacuate our home and stay with other relatives in Prescott. We did not have a generator; we had cold showers, cooked on the barbecue, and, at night, did almost everything by candlelight.

Kathy Putman, as told to Julie Putman
St. Joseph Catholic School • Prescott, Ontario

The 1998 Ice Storm hit nearly half of the Quebec population, leaving people without electricity from several days to several weeks. The Montreal area and the city of Montreal, as well as the south shore of Montreal and part of the Outaouais corridor, were particularly affected. Thousands of utility poles and transmission towers were crushed. The Joliette area was practically spared, although the schools were closed for two days. It is interesting to note that the Right Honourable Jean Chrétien was a student at our school (formerly Seminaire de Joliette) from 1946 to 1951.

Roger Desrochers, religion teacher
Academie Antoine-Manseau • Joliette, Quebec

Ontario Hydro to the Rescue

The Ice Storm of the week of January 5, 1998, devastated a large portion of the electrical distribution system operated by Ontario Hydro (now known as Power One) and local municipal utilities. Ontario Hydro executed a massive program to restore electricity supply to almost 150,000 of its customers, and over 122,000 customers of municipal utilities. The storm disabled 30 percent of the region's low-voltage electricity distribution system, requiring the replacement of more than 12,000 poles, 2,800 kilometres of conductor, and 83,500 insulators. It also damaged more than 100 high-voltage transmission towers, disrupted telephone and other electronic communications, and left road, rail, and air transportation at a virtual standstill.

At the height of the power restoration period, more than 3,000 staff members from Ontario Hydro, along with crews from Ontario municipal utilities and other utilities from Canada and some U.S. states, worked around the clock to rebuild the system. In addition, more than 3,500 Canadian Forces personnel performed valuable service in assisting with power restoration work. The direct cost of the storm to Ontario Hydro was approximately $135 million, while the overall cost to the region is estimated at $500 million.

— Al Manchee
Power One

CONSTRUCTION VOLUNTEERS CANADA

A volunteer and I are given a tour of Mt. Royal Park, Montreal, Quebec. There was extensive damage to this famous park.

supply services department creatively sourced out goods and services and acquired generators from New Brunswick, Quebec, Ontario, New York, Vermont, and Florida.

In the towns and villages that fill in the expanse of frozen terrain between the big cities, community spirit was in full force. St-Valentin, about 400 kilometres southeast of Montreal, near the Quebec–Vermont border, is a perfect example. When I arrived with a volunteer crew, it was wonderful to discover that people had come from even further away than we had: St-Valentin is twinned with Sakuto-Cho, Japan, who had already dispatched a group of townsfolk to help their Canadian brothers and sisters.

COURTESY, CONSTRUCTION VOLUNTEERS CANADA

Attending the Lovers Festival, St-Valentin, Quebec.

The area's economy is dependent on maple trees for its maple syrup production. When we arrived and saw such extensive damage, it looked like a lost cause. But we persevered. It is hard to describe how bone-numbingly difficult and relentless the work was in those conditions. Our bodies ached not only from the physical labour but also from the

I shiver, pulling my blankets up to
my cold nose.
The wind pounds on my window,
keeping me awake.
This nightmare of a storm is not even
letting me escape its wrath
in my dreams,
Trapping me in its icy reality.
Every day, I wait for my Knight in
shining armour.

Melika Laflamme
Hadley Junior High School
Hull, Quebec

OP RECUPERATION

During the Ice Storm of January 1998, 1 Wing was mobilized. Helicopters from all central and eastern squadrons were deployed where they were needed with little notice. OP RECUPERATION, the name given our relief effort, provided a unique opportunity to showcase the latest technology. With the direction of Hydro-Québec a 1 Wing crew from 430 ETAH dropped railroad ties and small logs onto the wires at night to knock ice off them. The CBC national news covered this first-of-its-kind mission. 1 Wing crews used the Forward Looking Infra Red (FLIR) sensor, which picks up heat signatures, to tell which lines had power, and which houses had candles, which had fireplaces, and which had wood stoves in operation. We covered large areas this way; ground troops followed up, ensuring the safety of isolated families.

— Air Force Association of Canada

COURTESY THE UNIVERSITY OF MONTREAL

City of Toronto Employees Pitch In

City of Toronto police, fire, ambulance, hydro, urban forestry, and works operations departments volunteered to take emergency equipment and supplies to relief centres in Ontario and Quebec.

Among the City of Toronto employees involved in the Ice Storm relief effort was Jason Doyle, a supervisor who works with arborists and tree pruners in Toronto. Jason recalls driving to Kingston with two fully equipped aerial tower crews before dawn on January 9, 1998:

"As the dawn broke, the devastation unfolded. It was unbelievable. The ice had produced a beautifully mesmerizing glass forest of woodlots along the highway. We proceeded with caution, but the roads and damage got worse. Kingston looked like a bomb had hit it. No hydro, no heat, and ice cold. Kingston staff were still reeling from the amount of damage and the huge task they faced."

A Toronto tree pruner prepares to chainsaw broken limbs hanging over a house and garage. — Courtesy City of Toronto

Jason and his crews were among many that arrived in the ensuing days to help restore electric power and remove hazards. The tree crews worked with a grid system based on priority.

"The crews quickly bonded as a team, a mixture of municipal and commercial climbers," says Jason. "They worked 14- to 18-hour days, starting at six each morning. They were there as volunteers helping a community in desperate circumstances. Their skill, professionalism, and compassion made me proud to be part of the arboriculture industry."

— Bob Langmaid,
City of Toronto

This was the kind of eerie scene encountered across rural and urban landscapes throughout eastern Ontario and southern Quebec after the ice storm of 1998.
— City of Toronto

The Ontario March of Dimes Marches In

Cold hands, warm hearts — not even the country's worst ice storm ever could deter the spirits of Ontario March of Dimes's staff and volunteers.

The Ontario March of Dimes provided assistance to George Funnel of the Ottawa–Brockville area, who requires help because of cerebral palsy. During the Ice Storm, his power and heat went out. Joe McMaster went beyond the call of duty.

"Joe came over and took us to his place because we had no power or heat," said George's mother, Molly Funnel. "Joe is a very compassionate man. He saw we were in difficulty and immediately helped us out."

"I never thought anything of it," said Joe.

The Funnels were not the only ones camping out in Joe's house — 12 people and three dogs crammed into Joe's two-bedroom home in Gananoque.

— Marsha Stephen,
Ontario March of Dimes

DND CANADA

Many Disasters Don't Have to Happen

We live in a world full of risks. As long as we've been on this planet, we have been subject to floods, tornadoes, earthquakes, landslides, and ice storms, as well as all the other natural hazards nature throws at us. But do natural disasters have to happen?

People can do a lot to reduce damage and loss of life that occurs when nature decides to go on a rampage. For instance, people who place themselves in harm's way will eventually be harmed. Many cities have been built in dangerous areas, near places where earthquakes and flooding often occur, for example. But even if we decide to develop in risky areas, we can build in such a way as to minimize the amount of damage that can occur when nature strikes. We can make houses flood- or earthquake-resistant, or listen to weather warnings, by knowing what to do when emergencies occur, by having emergency kits available, and by buying insurance. We can't stop nature's fury, but we can reduce our vulnerability.

— Dave Etkin, Environment Canada

searing pain of the cold temperatures, which often dipped below –10°C. The devastation that surrounded us added greatly to the burden.

Area youth showed stoicism beyond their years. They handled the disaster better than many of the adults, perhaps because they didn't have the worry of financial matters. Occasionally, you would catch a child trying to comfort a sobbing parent: "Mommy, don't cry. I'm fine. We didn't get hurt." Such acts of compassion were in themselves quiet acts of heroism.

If there is a lesson I learned from the Ice Storm, it is that joie de vivre is a powerful antidote for stressful times. In St-Valentin's case, the town was not going to let an ice storm derail one of its big tourist events — the annual Lovers Festival. Maple syrup may be vital to St-Valentin's

COURTESY, CONSTRUCTION VOLUNTEERS CANADA

Lending a helping hand to volunteers and a worker for the municipality of St-Valentin.

economy, but the Lovers Festival is its signature event. On February 14, a mere month after the storm had hit, the town welcomed about 5,000 visitors with the same festive and generous hospitality it had shown in previous years, undeterred by the ravages of the storm.

Back in Goulburn, Al Miley felt the same: "People who were coping with troubles of their own during the storm would sometimes invite us in for a meal. We were strangers, but they could see we were helping them. They were very gracious. It's not something you see in people in ordinary circumstances."

Year 1998, something to dread
Cold and fear enters our worlds
And we wait for warmth
A light to rely on.
Unbelieving, I watch from my window.

Bianca Baragoin
Richmond Regional High School
Richmond, Quebec

There was so much ice on the tree branches that they started to drop down. One of the branches was down so low it was touching a power line near our house. My dad saw this and knew it was dangerous. He was right. The branch started to smoke. A Hydro-Québec truck was driving by and saw what was happening. By this time the tree was on fire. The Hydro workers cut down the tree. Part of the tree landed on our doghouse. My dog started barking: Even though he wasn't in his house, he was still upset. My brother and I started throwing pails of water on the doghouse. My parents ran to get more water but by the time they got back we had the fire out. The Hydro men left and we were left with a burned down doghouse.

Tyler Maloney • Hadley Junior High School • Hull, Quebec

JOHN BOYD, NATIONAL ARCHIVES OF CANADA PA-70998

Sunnyside Avenue in Toronto after an ice storm, February 9, 1918.

CHAPTER 2

The Avalanche of Kangiqsualujjuaq, Quebec

New Year's Eve 1998–99

PAUL CHIASSON/CP

Shovels line the outside of the gymnasium of the school in Kangiqsualujjuaq, Quebec. An avalanche of snow from the hill behind the school slammed into it, killing nine people during a New Year's celebration.

FOR THE RECORD

- 600 people live in the Inuit village of Kangiqsualujjuaq in northern Quebec
- 9 people died, many of them children
- 150 children were left without winter outerwear
- the village school was heavily damaged and had to be rebuilt in a different location

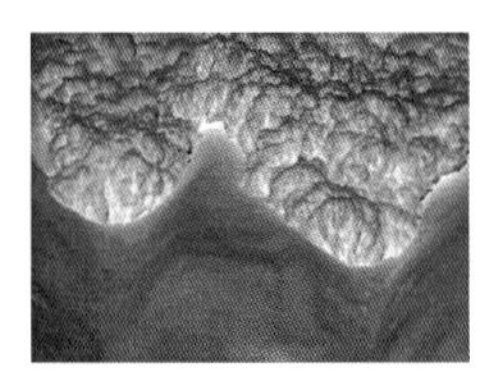

In Kangiqsualujjuaq, Quebec,
the avalanche came,
It took nine lives and left the pain.
No one knows the reason why,
All I know is we have to try
To lend a hand.

The emergency crews worked day and night,
The many names who gave their time
To heal and comfort those who grieve
With courage of heroic deeds
And helping hands.

Nine special people lost their lives,
And that made me realize
Communities are built by the things we do.
If we work together we'll pull through
By lending a hand.

(dedicated to the victims,
the victims' families, and volunteers)
Elise Lawton
Holy Rosary Catholic School,
Burlington, Ontario

AN IMAGE THAT WILL BE FOREVER IMPRINTED ON MY MIND IS THAT OF WAYNE ETOK, A five-year-old boy, looking out of his snow-rimmed window in Kangiqsualujjuaq, his arms hugging his tiny body in an effort to keep warm. He looked frightened, and no wonder: a deadly avalanche had ploughed through Satuumavik school at midnight on December 31, 1998, just as this tiny Inuit village was ringing in the New Year.

Kangiqsualujjuaq is located in northern Quebec on the east coast of Ungava Bay, at the mouth of the George River, 160 kilometres northeast of Kuujjuaq. It's a town of 600, a depressed village that rarely gets a chance to celebrate anything. When disaster struck that night, the town lost its most valuable asset — nine people, many of them children.

The sight of Wayne Etok motivated me to call the town to see if our newly formed organization, Construction Volunteers Canada, could be of assistance. But the township didn't need building materials — it needed winter clothing for 150 children between the ages of four and 12. When the avalanche struck, the children's snowsuits, mitts, hats, and boots were swept away. And so, CVC organized its first clothing drive. The media supported our appeal, and I was inundated with clothing donations from across the country. My house was filled to capacity with donations.

In the same way the image of Wayne Etok had inspired me to help, so too did the image of a hockey sweater draped over a small coffin inspire a young hockey team. The 11-year-old boys on the Atom AA hockey team at Toronto's Ted Reeve Arena collected warm clothing and sent it to the children in Kangiqsualujjuaq. On the condolence card accompanying their gift, the members signed their hockey sweater numbers beside their names. CVC appreciated the efforts of Wendy Fuller, who organized the clothing drive.

There were many similar gestures made to Kangiqsualujjuaq. A little girl sent her Angel Barbie as a gift to a child. In one of the most poignant letters I've read, an elderly gentleman sent his late daughter's coats: In his note he told me he had kept the coats for 23 years, ever since his 17-year-old daughter had died. He didn't want the coats to be sold, he wanted them donated and used. He was trusting us with this mission. The congregation of St. Andrew's Presbyterian Church in Aurora, Ontario, sent a sympathy card signed by its parishioners. Bev Mitchell knit mittens. "Each stitch is held with hugs and kisses," she wrote.

Anatomy of a Disaster: The Avalanche at Kangiqsualujjuaq

The night of December 31, 1998, was a night not of new beginnings but of tragic endings for the native village of Kangiqsualujjuaq in northern Quebec. At midnight, most of the 650 villagers were in the Satuumavik school gymnasium, ringing in the New Year with cheers and dancing, happy to be out of the blizzard that raged outside. Less than two hours later, their festivities were brought to a sudden halt by a thunderous crack. The walls were torn apart as an avalanche thundered through the school.

Those who were only partially buried began digging for their friends and families immediately, using their bare hands until some villagers were free to run for shovels. Those from neighbouring villages joined their efforts as the rescuers dug through 3 metres of snow and debris. The storm, and the village's remote location, delayed the arrival of emergency crews. When they did arrive, they treated those 25 who were injured, but nine more had already died from spinal injuries or suffocation. Half the wounded and five of the dead were children.

Avalanches are a hazard of mountain life in Canada. As wind and changing weather build increasingly unstable layers of snow on mountain peaks and crests, a change in temperature or a loud noise can cause a slab to break loose, thus triggering an avalanche. In 1998 in Kangiqsualujjuaq, heavy snowstorms built a massive ridge of snow at the crest, increasing the likelihood, and ultimately the damage, of an avalanche. Many feel that with the school's location only 300 meters from the foot of a steep, 150-metre-high ridge, this was a disaster waiting to happen.

Despite their deep sorrow, villagers are thankful that the avalanche didn't happen on a school day, when their losses could have been much greater; the classrooms, which faced the ridge, took the worst of the damage. They were filled to the ceilings with snow.

Over the past 12 years, there have been only two cases in Canada of avalanches causing deaths in residential areas, and those cases lead to the combined loss of three lives, more reason why the Kangiqsualujjuaq avalanche is so tragic. No less significant is the feeling that it might have been prevented even without the prohibitive expense of moving the school. After a smaller avalanche in 1994 buried one young man for 30 minutes before he was rescued unharmed, a report suggested to the Kativik school board that, while the school didn't appear to be threatened, erecting protective snow fences would be a wise cautionary measure. After the avalanche, officials were still uncertain whether snow fences would have saved the gym from an avalanche of this magnitude; subsequently an inquiry was commissioned to look into the subject. The people of Kangiqsualujjuaq will not be waiting for findings to act, however. They have identified 10 buildings around the town that they feel are too close to the hillside, and they have relocated all of them.

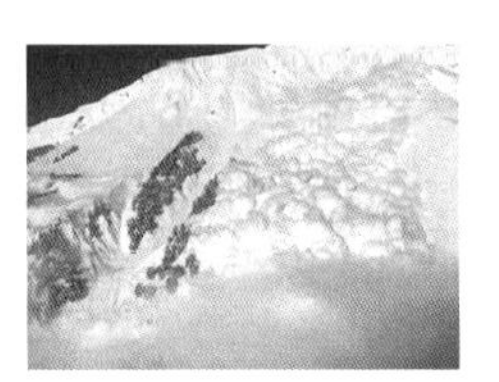

When disasters occur, many people have to give up their time to help rebuild roads and highways. It is important for young people to learn to serve their communities.

Jordan Morton
École W.S. Hawrylak School
Regina, Saskatchewan

In British Columbia there are many dormant volcanoes. These volcanoes could erupt at any time, so you should prepare just in case.

Stanley Chan
Waverley Elementary
Vancouver, British Columbia

A huge earthquake may release energy 10,000 times as great as an atomic bomb.

Justine Wong and Andrew Cheng
Waverley Elementary
Vancouver, British Columbia

HEALTH CANADA

The central depot of Health Canada. The National Emergency Stockpile System of Health Canada is made up of seven federal depots across Canada, 1,600 pre-positioned sites, and the central depot in Ottawa. The stockpile has everything that you would expect to find in a hospital, from beds and blankets to a supply of pharmaceuticals and a range of antibiotics. The supplies can be sent to a disaster area within 24 hours.

In the Vancouver area, most of the landslides are debris avalanches and flows. These happen because of heavy rains that fill the soil with water. The soil moves down the mountain slope and gets faster and faster as it grows in size. The result is destroyed property and damage near the bottom of the slope. In some places, such as Port Alice on Vancouver Island, dikes are made to keep out the debris. This helped protect the town from debris flows in 1973 and 1975.

Jasmine Louwe and Kenneth So
Waverley Elementary School,
Vancouver, British Columbia

In the end, we collected enough clothing to outfit Kangiqsualujjuaq four times over. And true to the town's request, 90 percent of the clothing was for children. CVC is grateful for donations supplied by Mark's Work Wearhouse, Swift Sure, Air Inuit, Purolator Courier, Muskoka Transit, First Air, Bi-Way, and Laycock's Dry Cleaners. Coats for Kids, another charity, also supplied clothing.

Of the many people who gave assistance to Kangiqsualujjuaq, the Junior Canadian Rangers stand out as unsung heroes.

The Rangers are comprised of 12- to 19-year-olds, mostly Inuit and First Nations. They are considered a true militia, not for their conventional military proficiency, but for their local knowledge, including survival skills. They are not trained at taxpayers expense; they have to know such skills before they are permitted to join.

The Junior Canadian Rangers program, officially created in 1996 by the Department of National Defence, stresses traditional culture and disciplines as well as modern life skills. Currently, there are 1,650 Junior Canadian Rangers in 61 patrols across northern, coastal, and isolated areas of Canada. They enjoy a variety of activities: hunting, fishing, living off the land, building sleds, canoes, and igloos, and learning about native spirituality, local dialects, and traditional songs and dances.

But in the aftermath of the Kangiqsualujjuaq avalanche, their courage was certainly tested. They assisted in digging out the school to retrieve the bodies of those who perished, and they worked around the clock to ensure the safety of the community. They built coffins — two of those killed were Rangers themselves — buried the dead, and helped empty houses that were threatened by the possibility of another avalanche.

During the Kangiqsualujjuaq avalanche, the children in the gym of the village school lost their outerwear, which was buried in the ice. Clothing was collected from across the country. One of the Ontario schools donated artwork.

Josh Wilcox
École W.S. Hawrylak School
Regina, Saskatchewan

COURTESY JUNIOR CANADIAN RANGERS

Junior Canadian Rangers

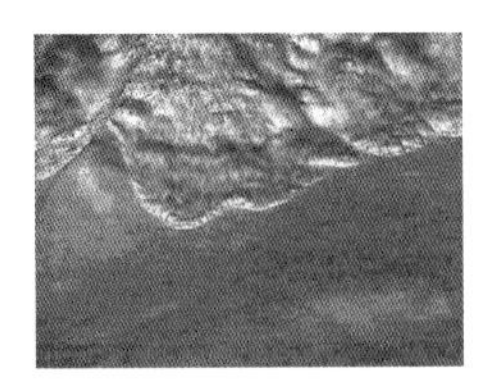

I have thought about solutions to prevent avalanches from hurting people. My solution would be to make signs that say, "Do not pass this point, avalanche in the area. Thank you." If that didn't work, I would tell the government that no more people should go where avalanches might happen because they might get killed.

Natalie Przeworski
Waverley Elementary School
Vancouver, British Columbia

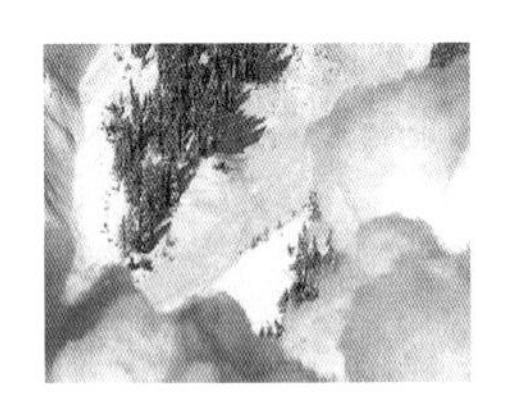

On April 29, 1903, at 4:10 a.m., 30 million cubic meters of limestone fell from the top of Turtle Mountain and buried a part of the sleeping town of Frank, Alberta. The rock mass was 150 meters deep, 425 meters high, and 1,000 meters wide. The town of Frank was home to 600 people; 100 people were in the path of the slide, and about 70 died.

Adrianne Humen
Byron Northview Public School
London, Ontario

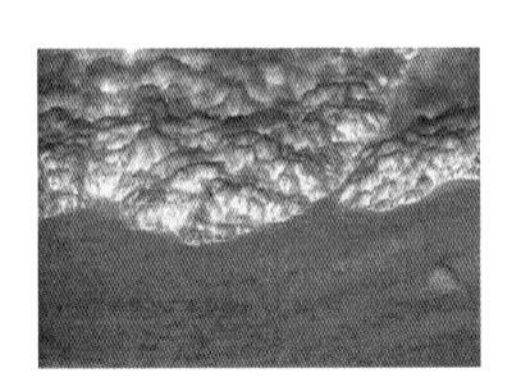

Landslides, rock avalanches
Crash down the mountain slope,
Leaving innocent people
Buried without any hope.
In 1959 in Pandemonium Creek, B.C.,
The landslide debris
Reached speeds of 360 km per hour,
A frightful sight to see.

(dedicated to the Canadians lost in landslides)
Gita Singh
Morning Star Middle School
Mississauga, Ontario

That's a lot of responsibility for a young group.

Other avalanches — not always the snowy variety — have struck Canada in recent years.

In May 1971, in the company town of Saint-Jean-Vianney, Quebec, more than 30 people, most of them children, were sucked into a sinkhole, along with 34 homes and dozens of cars and buses. All this was accomplished in less than five minutes.

In June 1993, the land where the town of Lemieux, Ontario, had been situated collapsed into the South Nation River, creating a new bay in the process. Fortunately, the government had dismantled the town two years before, after a geological survey revealed that the land was at risk. Because of this initiative, many lives were saved when the inevitable collapse occurred.

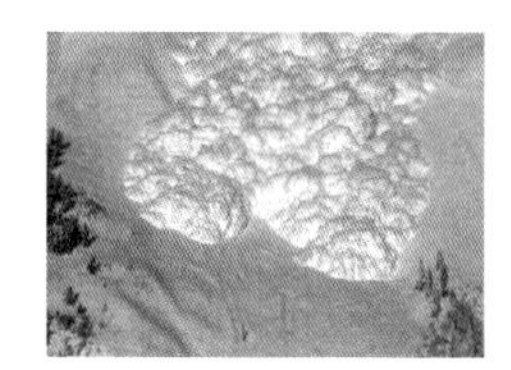

We are small and weak when compared with Mother Nature, a force that is stronger than everything, a strength that can penetrate any wall, house, or shield.

Agnieszka Grudniewicz
St. Patrick's Intermediate School
Ottawa, Ontario

NATIONAL ARCHIVES OF CANADA/PA23921

The Quebec Citadel landslide, September 19, 1889.

When a volcano erupts, some of the rocks melt in the explosion, making lava.

Adrien Ip
Waverley Elementary
Vancouver, British Columbia

Earthquakes are caused when the earth's planes move on top of each other. Earthquakes can destroy anything.

Michelle Wong
Waverley Elementary
Vancouver, British Columbia

THE FRANK SLIDE

In the year 1903, a horrible event took place in the tiny town of Frank, Alberta. Frank was a mining town known primarily for its production of coal. Coal was used as a major source of heat at the time and it provided the region with power.

In the spring of 1903, there were deep rumblings in the rock. Some of the timbers lining the tunnel began to heave and crack.

At 4 o'clock in the morning on April 29, 17 men who were working the night shift were digging at the coal face far below the surface. A roar fell over the tunnel. Timbers split like match sticks. The mine filled with dust.

The 17 men started to climb the slope to the entrance 100 feet away but their way was blocked by a thick wall of rock. They tried the air shaft but found the tunnel to the shaft also obstructed. Their only hope was to dig through the wall of rock. After a few hours, a small ray of light was visible. When the men came out of the mine, they expected to see their homes, but all they saw was a rock pile 45 feet high.

While most of the townsfolk were fast asleep, a rock slide began and moved so quickly, there was no time to escape, no warning. In just over a minute and a half, 90 million tons of rock had roared more than half a mile down the mountainside and thundered across the valley. Nobody in its path had an opportunity to run out of harm's way.

One of the survivors from the mine was able to prevent another disaster by signalling a train to stop before it collided with a big wall of rock.

Highway 3, the route that leads from Lethbridge, Alberta, through to the Crowsnest Pass, runs over this enormous grey rock blanket that covered the valley. Tourists today can read a plaque whose words tell of the 66 people who died in the Frank slide and now lie beneath these travellers' feet.

— Ritche Holm,
Canadian Martyrs Catholic School,
Oshawa, Ontario

There are three kinds of avalanches: A dry snow avalanche made of powder and air moves faster than 160 km per hour. A wet snow avalanche is made of wet snow, and it moves a bit slower. A slab avalanche happens when a piece of snow breaks loose as a big chunk and breaks into many pieces as it slides down the mountain. One of the most famous avalanches in Canada was the avalanche that took the life of former prime minister Pierre Trudeau's son Michel, who was skiing on Mount Logan in Kokanee Glacier Park. His body was never recovered.

Jessica Yuen and Alex Dam
Waverley Elementary School
Vancouver, British Columbia

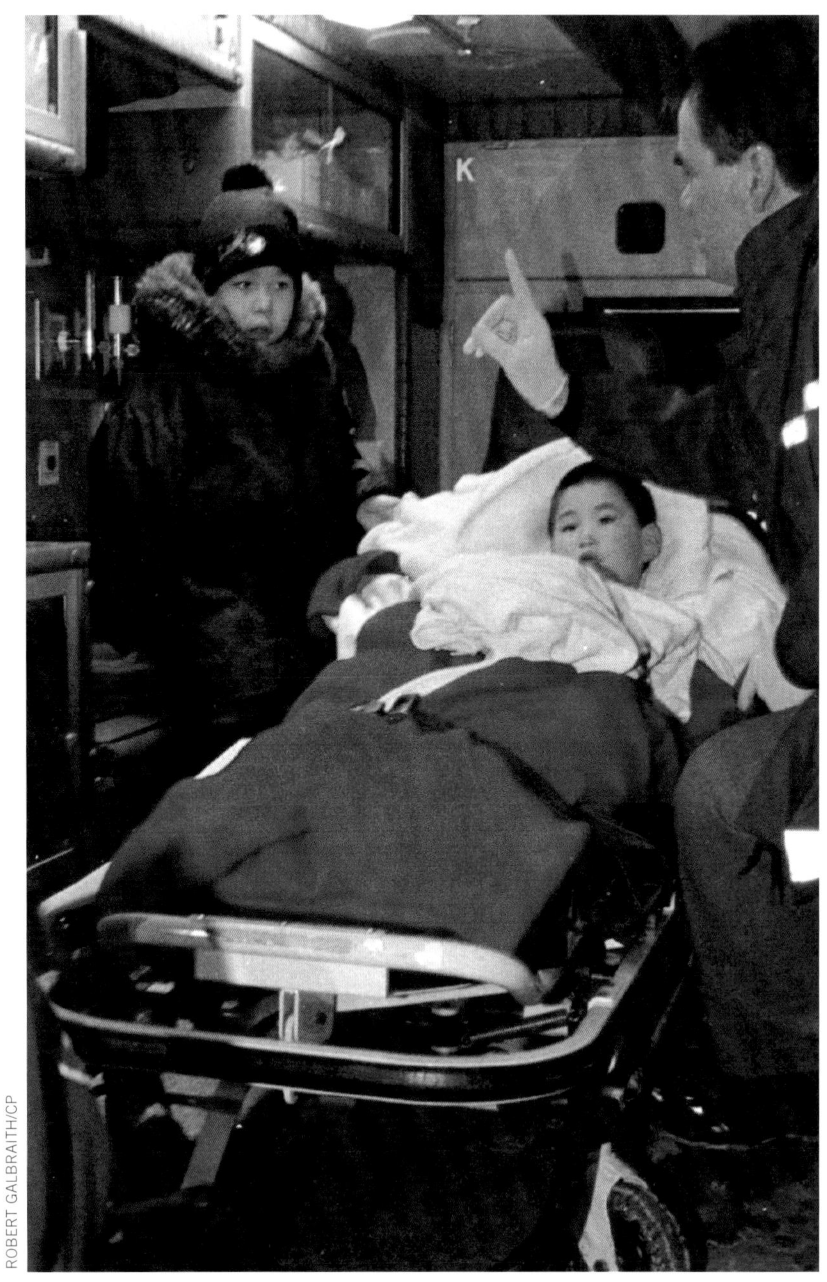

ROBERT GALBRAITH/CP

Two young Inuit boys are escorted to the emergency doors of a Montreal hospital after suffering injuries in the avalanche in Kangiqsualujjuaq, Quebec.

Royal Canadian Mounted Police / Gendarmerie royale du Canada

news release

FOR IMMEDIATE DISTRIBUTION

Revelstoke RCMP File#: 2003-257

February 2, 2003
Time released: 4:00 pm

Update: Seven Students Killed In Tragic Avalanche

Revelstoke, BC: The investigations continue into the tragic death of seven Alberta teens killed Saturday in an avalanche.

17 back country skiers (three adults, 14 students) were caught in an avalanche while skiing up the Balu Pass Trail along Connaught Creek in Glacier National Park around 11:45 am on Saturday February 1st.

Investigators have been on the scene today gathering information. The area where the avalanche occurred remains closed and will not open until the investigation is concluded. More than a dozen investigators, from the RCMP, BC Coroner, and Parks Canada are involved and they are looking at all aspects surrounding this incident.

The preliminary investigative findings strongly suggest that this tragic, fatal avalanche was a naturally occurring event in nature. There is no suggestion to date that the avalanche was caused or created by a human source. The RCMP continues to assist the BC Coroner's office in its own investigation. The Coroner has determined that the seven individuals killed died of asphyxiation and it is still unknown whether a Coroner's inquest or inquiry will be called.

At this time, the RCMP can confirm the names of seven individuals, one female and six males killed. They were all 15 years old, from Calgary and were Grade 10 students of Strathcona-Tweedsmuir School located south of Calgary.

All of the families of the deceased have been contacted and arangements are being made to return the victims to their hometown.

Of the 10 survivors, one student sustained a leg injury, he was treated and released, and the nine other survivors were recovered without injury. The survivors of the group have provided statements to investigators and late this morning they all left the Revelstoke area. Victim's Services and grief counsellors here and in Alberta continue to work with the families of deceased to help them deal with this tragic event.

The RCMP would like to once again commend the various individuals and agencies who responded to the avalanche site. It was the quick and decisive efforts by the local ski guides, park wardens, helicopter pilots, avalanche experts and various other emergency personnel that saved and recovered the skiers and prevented further injuries and loss of life.

The Revelstoke RCMP recognizes the impact that this tragedy has had on the community, which is still dealing with events of last month's fatal avalanche and will continue to work with all parties directly and indirectly impacted.

===

Officials in Attendance:

Sgt. Grant Learned - Moderator RCMP Media/Communications
Sgt. Art Kleinsmith, NCO i/c Revelstoke RCMP Detachment
Pat Dunn, Communications Officer - Parks Canada
Mark McKee - Mayor of Revelstoke

- 30 -

Released by:

Sgt. Art Kleinsmith
NCO i/c Revelstoke Detachment

Royal Canadian Mounted Police / Gendarmerie royale du Canada

news release / communiqué

FOR IMMEDIATE DISTRIBUTION / POUR DIFFUSION IMMÉDIATE

Revelstoke RCMP Media Briefing
11:00hrs January 21, 2003

Current Status:

Revelstoke RCMP are still continuing their investigation into this tragic accident that occurred at 7600 feet in the area of the Durand Glacier.

Due to weather conditions police have not been able to gain access to the lodge where the police investigators and ski tour group are staying:

This is a synopsis of the events that transpired yesterday.

- Accident occurred shortly before 1100hrs PST
- Owner of Selkirk Mountain Experience who is with ski group calls to Selkirk Mountain Ski base to advise that an avalanche has just occurred and that numerous people involved.
- 11:38 PST Search and Rescue - Golden is called and fly to accident site
- Selkirk Mountain Helicopters send helicopter with several guides from Revelstoke to site
- BC Ambulance arrives at scene at 12:47. Delayed due to in climate weather. All victims had been rescued and ambulance personnel conducted examinations on scene.
- Survivors ferried via helicopter to Selkirk Mountain Experience Lodge
- 14:15hrs PST victims transported to Revelstoke and examined by Advanced Life support paramedics. Extraction of the victim took three flights.
- 14:45 PST RCMP investigators arrive at accident scene.
- 16:00 hrs PST RCMP start to contact authorities in Canada and the United States to notify the next of kin.

Sgt. Randy Brown
Media Liaison Officer

Royal Canadian Mounted Police / Gendarmerie royale du Canada

news release / communiqué

FOR IMMEDIATE DISTRIBUTION / POUR DIFFUSION IMMÉDIATE

Revestoke RCMP January 22, 2003
10:00 A.M
File 2003-00158 Durand Glacier Avalanche Accident

Update

Revelstoke RCMP and the BC Coroners Service are continuing their investigation into the tragic back country skiing accident that took seven lives on Monday January 20th, 2003.

RCMP investigators who were in and at the accident scene and area over the past two days returned last evening. They have met with the Coroners service and provided an initial assessment and overview of their preliminary investigation. The Coroner's service still has his avalanche investigators at the scene conducting snow surveys. There is nothing in the initial investigation at this time to lead investigators to believe that this is nothing other than a tragic accident that occurred on Monday morning. The coroners investigation and report is expected to take several months during which time the Coroner will determine if he will hold an inquest or inquiry into this event.

The remaining four skiers involved in the accident will be remaining at the Selkirk Mountain Experience Ski Lodge until Saturday.

Sgt. Randy Brown
Media Liaison Officer

Sgt. Art Kleinsmith
NCO i/c Revelstoke RCMP Detachment

CHAPTER 3

The Floods:

Saguenay, Lanark, Leamington, Huntsville, Haliburton, and Manitoba

DND CANADA

The Manitoba flood of 1997.

FOR THE RECORD

- 3 died in the Manitoba floods
- 10 died in Saguenay, Quebec
- 200,000 hectares of farmland were damaged in Manitoba
- 28,000 Manitobans were forced to leave their homes
- $100 million in damage was caused by the floods in Saguenay, Quebec

I have been really lucky during my life. I have never been in a natural disaster. I have contributed to needy people a few times. I gave canned food to Manitoba flood victims.

Jeff Rance
École W.S. Hawrylak School
Regina, Saskatchewan

THE DESTRUCTION BEGINS IMPERCEPTIBLY, ALMOST INNOCENTLY. A FEW days of rain and the ground is soggy underfoot. But how much rain has accumulated, and how soaked was the ground to begin with? If the water table is already high, disaster is imminent. As the water rises, so does the panic. All is quiet except for the eerie groans of structures vainly resisting the force of the floods. As quietly as they arrived, the waters recede, leaving unimaginable damage.

Ever since we first heard the story of Noah and the ark, floods have held an ominous fascination, a mixture of fear, awe, and fatalism. For those who have found themselves in the midst of a deluge, it is hard to imagine the day when life will return to normal. Until then, all they can do is wait for the water to go away, so they can start the laborious task of rebuilding their homes, and then their lives.

DND CANADA

Anatomy of a Disaster: Floods

Since ancient times, riverside dwellers have come to expect spring floods as a natural part of winter melt-off. In Canada, our ability to tame our rivers with dams and dikes has encouraged us to forget the destructive power of a flood. However, when unprecedented and unpredicted storms swell these rivers beyond our abilities to restrain them, they can become entities of relentless destruction, forcing people to escape their homes or be washed away along with them.

For the inhabitants of the Lac-St-Jean-Saguenay region of Quebec, 1996 will be remembered as the year their sense of security was washed away with the tides. Four miniature hurricanes travelling together from the south settled over the region from July 18 to 21, dropping up to 200 mm of rain in 36 hours. The downpour pooled in, overflowed the network of reservoirs, dikes, and dams throughout the region, and unleashed rolling torrents of water upon the towns. Waterlogging destabilized the sensitive clay soil, leading to landslides that, together with accidents caused by the flood, killed 10 people throughout the region. In total, the storm left over $800 million in damages. Approximately 16,000 people had to be evacuated, and many returned to find their homes in ruins (488 homes were destroyed and 1,230 were damaged).

Until the Red River flooded less than a year later, the 1996 Saguenay flood was called the worst in Canadian history. It's doubtful that even the experts expected the Red River to top the Saguenay when they began predicting in February that spring floods could be worse than usual that year. Then an early April snowstorm dumped about half a metre of snow into the Red River basin, and emergency crews had to react fast.

Working 24 hours a day for six days, workers and volunteers built the 40-km Brunkild Dike to the southwest of Winnipeg, but they couldn't protect most of the valley. The army arrived on April 21, and evacuations began the next day. By April 27, the river was already 60 cm to 1.2 m above its record height, set in 1979. By May 7, the flood area covered 2,000 square kilometres and was 30 km across at its widest. On May 16, more than 25,000 Manitobans were still waiting to go home.

While later floods in Leamington, Huntsville, and Haliburton, Ontario, and Vanguard, Saskatchewan, were not nearly as far-reaching or catastrophic as the floods of 1996 and 1997, they were still damaging to the people they affected. These floods resulted in the loss of property and the risk of loss of life, as well as damage to homes, farmers' fields and crops, and the water supplies of the towns.

DND CANADA

Members of 3 Princess Patricia's Canadian Light Infantry, Edmonton, and Lord Strathcona's Horse (Royal Canadian), Edmonton, help build a dike in the North Kildonon area, Manitoba. The street dike was a secondary precaution to the river dike, which is 45 metres in front of it.

During the Red River flood, the City of Winnipeg asked the Salvation Army to help provide temporary housing and distribution of food. The Salvation Army mobilized 30 mobile centres, canteen trucks, and other vehicles from across Canada and the United States. They organized food preparation and delivered meals to volunteers at sandbagging sites and to residents in emergency shelters. Hundreds of tons of donated clothing, food, and other goods from across Canada were processed in large warehouses for distribution. Once the flood waters receded, Salvation Army volunteers visited people as they returned to their homes, gave them supplies, and helped them get their lives back on track. By the summer, the Salvation Army began rebuilding communities. Families whose homes were totally destroyed received a grant of $2,500; families whose homes were extensively damaged received $1,250. Throughout the fall and winter of 1997 and the spring of 1998, the Salvation Army sponsored dinners and community meetings to bolster the spirits of those still struggling to recover.

— Jim Ferguson, Territorial Emergency Disaster Services Director, Salvation Army

GREG BROOKS, GEOLOGICAL SURVEY OF CANADA

The town of Morris, surrounded by river waters during the May 1997 Red River flood. The ground surface in the town is lower than the level of flooding. A ring-dike formed by a narrow mound of earth surrounding the town prevented the flood waters from inundating the town.

Days and weeks before the flood, people put sandbags around their houses. Some people were very frightened. Some animals that didn't know how to swim drowned. A young boy was sucked into a drain. Many people were injured and became sick. Houses were flooded. Some people lost something they treasured or had had for a long time. During the flood, I lost something I had ever since I was born. It was a Winnie the Pooh bear. When I was seven years old, the flood washed it away.

Alyssa Galon
Lord Nelson School
Winnipeg, Manitoba

It can take years to fully repair the distress inflicted by a single flood. As Sylvie Poirier, a social worker with CLSC du Fjord in La Baie, Quebec, acknowledges, "For the [victims] who suffered losses in the flood (human, psychological, material) the process [of returning to normal life] was much harder and slower. Some people still experienced post-traumatic symptoms five years after."

Several major floods have recently taken their toll on the Canadian landscape.

The first occurred in 1996, when the Saguenay River and Lac St-Jean in eastern Quebec, swollen from a two-day rainfall, flooded over and spilled across the already soggy soil. Terra

Many organizations, such as the Salvation Army, sent food, clothing, and household articles. The government gave $100,000 to homeowners to repair or rebuild. These events teach us to be thankful for the people and things in our lives, and never to take life for granted. They also teach us to help those who are in need because you never know, one day you might need help, too.

Edyta Danowska
Ascension of Our Lord Secondary School
Mississauga, Ontario

CITY OF WINNIPEG

A 24-hour patrol monitors a sandbag dike, checking for stability and potential leakage.

DND CANADA

In April 1997, flood reports for cities along the Red River valley in North and South Dakota foretold a serious threat to Canadians. As the rising waters flowed north to Manitoba, civil authorities scrambled to protect threatened communities. Before long, the Manitoba government called on the military for assistance, and the relief operation eventually involved over 9,000 Canadian Forces personnel. 1 Wing team was heavily involved from the start. From Edmonton, 408 Squadron formed the core of a 1 Wing aviation component that flew more than 700 hours during the operation. The unit managed to muster five aircrews and technicians from Valcartier and dispatch them to augment 408 Squadron. The tactical aviation community of 1 Wing took up the challenge of the flood and went head to head with rising waters, rescuing stranded people and herding wandering livestock. Despite the difficulties presented by a new aircraft and new operating procedures, 1 Wing aircrew, technicians, and support personnel kept the Griffon flying, day and night, for the entire operation. Were they successful? Ask any Manitoban!

— Air Force Association of Canada

firma turned into a bog and mammoth mudslides resulted. In one of the more tragic incidents, a 10-year-old girl and her eight-year-old brother in Grande-Baie were killed when a saturated hill behind their home suddenly collapsed and poured into the basement bedrooms where the children were sleeping. They had no chance to escape.

In all, 10 people died and more than 20,000 homes were destroyed. Amid the chaos and catastrophic loss, volunteers sprang into action. Saint Vincent de Paul, Chicoutimi, Montreal, Quebec City, and the Provincial Council of Quebec gathered food, furniture, and clothing. Members of St. John Ambulance Division 1034 in Chicoutimi and the Chicoutimi police helped 16,000 people flee their homes, while St. John Ambulance workers in Jonquière administered first aid and helped settle the growing waves of evacuees. The local Holiday Inn also administered first aid.

You should help your community at any age. Though I have not experienced flooding, in a way I wish I had so I could prove to people that I am willing to help out others as much as possible.

Kristen Marbach
École W.S. Hawrylak School
Regina, Saskatchewan

DND CANADA

The 1997 Manitoba flood.

NATIONAL ARCHIVES OF CANADA/C3592

Spring inundation, Montreal, Quebec, 1865.

COURTESY *RED RIVER VALLEY ECHO*

Mennonite children in Rosenort, Manitoba, hitch a ride on a sandbag wagon during the flood of 1997.

In an essay about the flood that terrorized their town, two students, Marie-Eve Larouche and Marie-Hélène Dion of École St. Alphonse in La Baie, Quebec, wrote about the two children who were killed in the basement of their home and about a small house that symbolized the flood: "A small, solid house that everyone has seen on the news and no one can forget represents the spirit of the people to overcome this disaster. While everything around it was carried away, the little house stood its ground and resisted the violent flood waters."

Evacuees were given shelter at Bagotville Military Air Base. "Teams of military personnel from Bagotville, Valcartier, and Montreal evacuated 3,760 people," said sub-lieutenant Luc Charron.

People were not the only ones helped: A group of dogs, cats, rabbits, ferrets, and budgies were cared for and fed by Sergeant Richard Métivier and soldiers from the 12th régiment blindé du Canada of Valcartier when an animal shelter was lost to the flood.

Although $100 million was sustained in damages, Jean Tremblay, the mayor of Chicoutimi, estimates the disaster will have cost Canadians and Quebecers nearly half a billion dollars.

The next year, the flood scene shifted west.

GREG BROOKS, GEOLOGICAL SURVEY OF CANADA

The Chute-Garneau dam on Chicoutimi River, Saguenay Valley, Quebec, several days after the July 1996 Saguenay floods. A newly eroded channel carried the flow beside the dam, completely bypassing the dam penstocks and sluice gates. The dam appeared undamaged, but it was unable to generate hydro-electric power because of the diverted flow. The new channel was formed when flood waters overtopped the dam and eroded the sediments beside it.

I saw the flood up close. The water was rising, and the radio announcers were telling people in our area to find a safer place. My family and I drove to St. Bernadette's Church in Ferand-Boileau. There was water coming up to the car windows. When we arrived at the church, there were a lot of people there. Later, helicopters took us to La Baie town hall. Then we went to the Bagotville military base in La Baie. At the base, we were housed and fed. We stayed there for about five days.

Jennilie Gagnon-Vincent
École St. Alphonse School
La Baie, Quebec

DND CANADA

DND CANADA

Corporal Odding (top) and Sergeant Miller of 2 Combat Engineering Regiment, Petawawa, help a small child down from the back of a M113 Dozer in the Kildonan area during the Manitoba Flood.

At first, it seemed like the Red River was going to win this one, but after an hour or two it seemed like we were gaining ground. Some people worked for hours and hours but the river was still rising. After the water receded, it seemed the damage was phenomenal. I was glad I could help out by stacking sandbags which kept some of the water back where it belonged.

Yifan Wong,
École W.S. Hawrylak School,
Regina, Saskatchewan

The Red River Flood of 1997 — the "Flood of the Century" — at least came with some warning: Manitobans had been following the havoc in Grand Forks, North Dakota, due south of their province, where the dikes had been easily overpowered as the river bulldozed its way through the centre of the city. Southern Manitoba had a flood plan in place, but it was clear that plan would be no match for what was to come. Dikes were hastily built; millions of sandbags were ordered and student volunteers were put on standby to fill them.

One such group of students, from Philemon Wright High School, travelled 4,444 kilometres by bus (Greyhound donated their bus fares) from Hull, Quebec, to Winnipeg just to help out. During one encounter, the students met a family whose home had been flooded by the storm.

CPL MIKE BARLEY/DND CANADA

Soldiers from 2 Princess Patricia's Canadian Light Infantry, Winnipeg, travel by boat to give out evacuation notices in the Grande Point area as Manitoba floodwaters continue to rise.

COURTESY MARJ HEINRICHS, ROSENORT, MANITOBA

Filling sandbags in Rosenort, Manitoba.

CPL MIKE BARLEY/DND CANADA

Members of the Royal 22e Régiment of Valcartier help build a dike in St. Adolphe, south of Winnipeg.

DND CANADA

If I had a chance, I would have babysat for the children and families who lost their homes in the Manitoba floods. I would have done this for no charge because those families would have needed help.

Whitney Eberle
École W.S. Hawrylak School,
Regina, Saskatchewan

The CRWRC and the Manitoba Flood

One of the most difficult and back-breaking jobs after a flood is the clean-up, pumping out and cleaning up the basements, taking water-soaked furniture and other house contents outside, and removing drywall from the studs. The Christian Reformed World Relief Committee of Canada (CRWRC) worked for two years after the flood with the Mennonite Disaster Response Services, repairing and rebuilding homes. This was a fine example of Christians coming together to serve people in need.

— Jacob Kramer
Christian Reformed World Relief
Committee of Canada

The family had two teenagers and was sleeping at a senior citizens residence waiting to go home. The group watched a video showing the father's visit by boat to check out their home. Only the roof showed above the water. The students gave the family $1,005, money they had raised to pay for their trip.

Among countless other volunteer efforts, the St. Vincent de Paul Society sent nearly $175,000, and the RCMP's D Division raised $58,000 for a flood relief fund in addition to an extensive contribution of food, clothing, shelter, materials, equipment, and tireless labour. Of this money, $20,000 was donated to the Mennonite Disaster Service, which helped more than 800 families. More than 360 Navy diving teams plus Naval Reservists worked around the clock on dike reinforcement. Crews of 33 aircraft and 1,600 members of the Air Force maintained airborne communications for Griffon and Sea King helicopters, which used their digital imaging technology to probe the floodwaters. The Kinsmen Club of St. Albert, Alberta, organized the "Kin Ride to Low Tide," which brought 242

In the Red River Rampage of 1950, Lawson Alfred Ogg was one of the many volunteers to fill bags with sand and build a wall of these bags around the greater part of Winnipeg. Suddenly, the temperature dropped to freezing, a great gust of wind whipped the water against the sandbags, and one by one they burst open. The flood also burst open the door of Lawson's house and swept him down his stairs to the basement, where he died. Lawson was the only Winnipegger who died in that terrible flood.

Caylen and Marta Heckel
Prince Philip Public School
Niagara Falls, Ontario

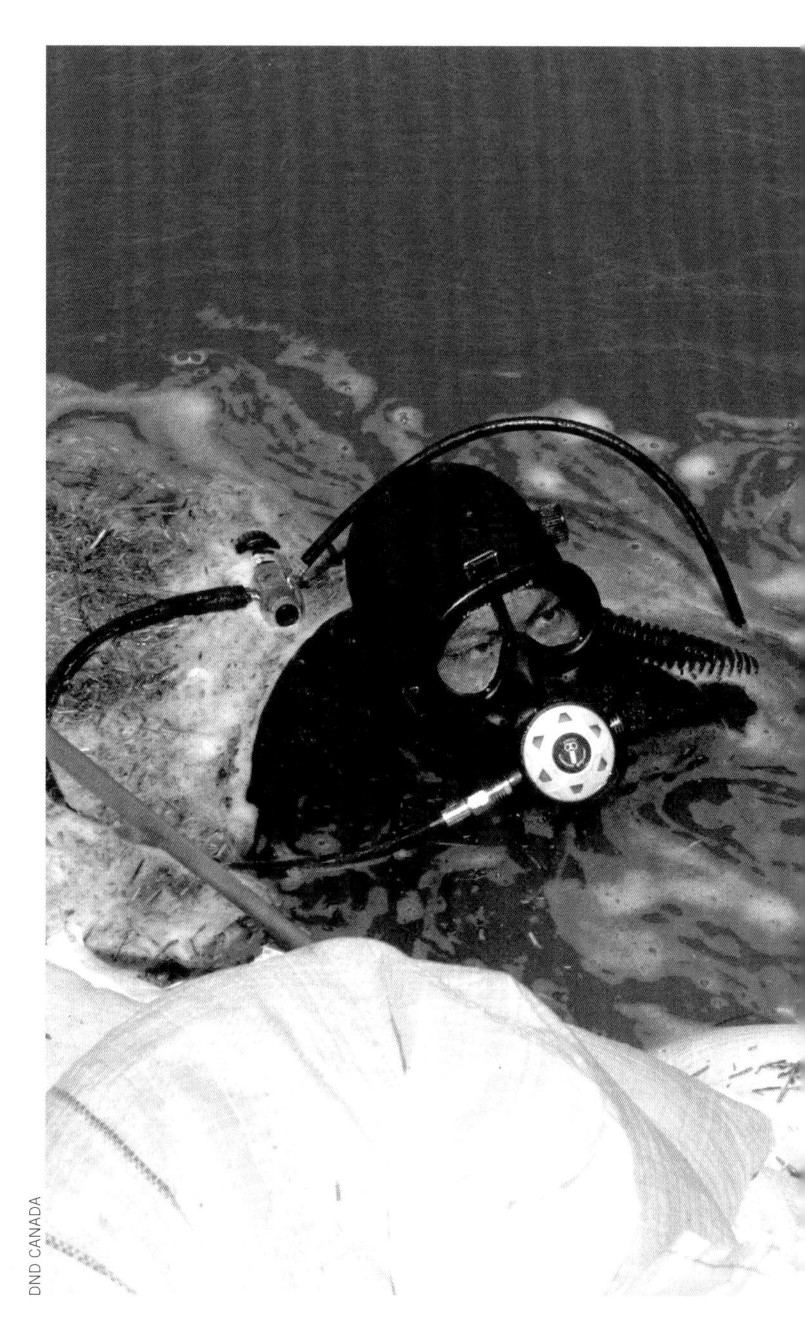
DND CANADA

DND CANADA

During the flood of 1997, brave Manitobans got together with the soldiers to save homes, especially those built near the river and in the valley. When the flood crested in Winnipeg, more than 28,000 people, 2,000 cattle, and 45,000 chickens had been evacuated. A decision had to be made to save the city, and the floodway was opened. Unfortunately, this ended up flooding an area about the size of Prince Edward Island — 2,000 square kilometres. This caused two communities to be flooded out — Ste. Agathe and Grande Pointe.

Katie Smith and Ms. Danya Jaworsky (teacher)
Lord Nelson School
Winnipeg, Manitoba

Kinsmen, Kinettes, and Kin friends from across Canada to the flood-ravaged area for four weeks to assist in the clean-up. A small Masonic lodge in the Ottawa Valley also chipped in their services. St. John Ambulance, as a diversionary tactic, offered flood evacuees a free 3.5-hour Life Saver program to take their minds off their water-logged predicament.

In the end, it was the volunteer effort that resulted in a triumph over tragedy. As Glen Murray, the mayor of Winnipeg, recounted: "It is estimated there were 150,000 volunteer days of work contributed to the flood fight. City crews and volunteers filled more than six million sandbags. If you put these six million sandbags end to end, they would stretch from Winnipeg to Vancouver."

The next year, on April 9, 1998, a flood hit Leamington, Ontario, population 12,000. By the time it was over, Essex County and neighbouring Pelee Island had sustained $5 million damage.

DND CANADA

Soldiers from 3 Princess Patricia's Canadian Light Infantry, Edmonton, check out a farm in the flood zone near the town of St. Agathe, Manitoba.

NATIONAL ARCHIVES OF CANADA/PA120378

The Penticton Creek flood, Penticton, British Columbia, May 1, 1942.

DND CANADA

The Coast Guard observes the flood damage.

I really enjoy helping out my community because it makes me feel happy when I have supported the less fortunate. When I think about it, I am truly very lucky. I haven't had any natural disasters happen to my home or to the homes of my friends.

Randall Brady
École W.S. Hawrylak School,
Regina, Saskatchewan

DND CANADA

COURTESY, CONSTRUCTION VOLUNTEERS CANADA

We invited the Salvation Army to a Christmas party held for victims of the Leamington flood.

After contacting Emergency Management Ontario to offer our help, I called the township council in nearby Mersea. The township gave me a list of some of the people hardest hit by the flood, and then I began dialling.

Some people might find it awkward to call people who are in distress. I don't. In addition to finding out what they need, I try to comfort people. Human contact is vital when a disaster occurs. People are vulnerable, and when they have no one to turn to they feel angry, fearful, and desperate. They often cry on the phone. Emotional help is just as critical as financial and physical help.

DND CANADA

COURTESY MARJ HEINRICHS, ROSENORT, MANITOBA

DND CANADA

DND CANADA

In speaking to the people of Leamington, I learned that, while the area was prone to flooding, this was one of the worst incidents in recent memory. I telephoned several tradesmen in and around the town and was encouraged to discover that many of them were already volunteering their time and skills. The mayor's office played a major role in determining the victims' needs.

Although I was involved in getting thousands of dollars in assistance to the victims of Leamington, I didn't get to the town immediately because I was involved in another disaster. When I did arrive, I couldn't believe what I saw: Floors had buckled and cracked with the rising levels, water had stained the walls, furnaces and electrical systems had been destroyed, breakwalls had crumbled.

It was clear the clean-up was going to be a mammoth undertaking. Construction Volunteers Canada provided assistance over a period of several months.

DND CANADA

DND CANADA

A convoy of Canadian Forces vehicles in Manitoba.

DND CANADA

Overseeing rescue operations from the air.

DND CANADA

Cleaning up a cemetery.

I feel good when I volunteer because I know that I've made a difference in somebody's life. There are many things you can do to help less fortunate people. You can pack up boxes and give clothes to the Salvation Army, who collects clothing for victims of natural disasters.

John Disbery
École W.S. Hawrylak School
Regina, Saskatchewan

Being an outsider has an advantage: You can see exactly what needs to be done. Those in the thick of things are often overwhelmed by the task ahead. And so, I waded in. Being from Toronto, I was found to be tenacious. But, undeterred, I encouraged people to help their neighbours, and paired those who were elderly and alone with younger families.

Not that the young ones were any better off than the older ones. One single mother was determined to renovate her house, which had been badly damaged. A couple with young children lost their home and eventually became destitute. Individuals were burdened by $50,000 damage to their homes, sometimes more — most, if not all of it, not covered by insurance.

When you live on the edge of a lake or a river, flooding is a real possibility. It goes with the territory. Some people think that if you are reckless enough to live on a flood plane you shouldn't expect compensation when it inevitably floods, but when someone is hurt, you don't sit back and justify it. You offer help.

But my experience has been that no one "expects" help: Every person our organization assisted was surprised and truly grateful for a helping hand. And when you extend a helping hand to someone, it in turn encourages them to help others. A chain reaction of compassion is created.

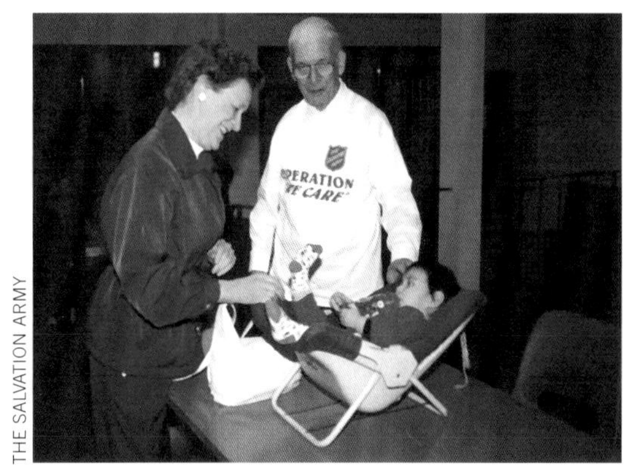

THE SALVATION ARMY

Salvation Army volunteer Les Sutton helps out a small flood victim in Morris, Manitoba.

DND CANADA

CPL ERIC JOLIN/DND CANADA

A convoy of 130 military vehicles drives down Winnipeg's streets as people come out to say thanks to the military for their efforts during the flood. The convoy was loaded onto trains and returned to 2 Royal Canadian Horse Artillery in Petawawa, Ontario.

Making Sure Money Goes Where It's Needed the Most

The Treasury Board of Canada helps manage money for the Canadian government. We make sure that the government spends money on the right things and on projects that help Canadians. That is why, when a major natural disaster strikes, the Treasury Board goes into action!

When a disaster, such as a flood or an ice storm, occurs, the Treasury Board's main job is to make sure there is enough money to buy blankets and food and other things to keep people safe. Treasury Board employees work with the provincial governments to figure out exactly how much money is needed. Over the last few years, emergency money has helped families rebuild houses and have helped people fix damaged stores.

— Treasury Board of Canada

DND CANADA

On May 3, 1991, there was a flood in Old Crow, Yukon. Old Crow is above the Arctic Circle. Half the town was asleep; the other half was watching the ice jam up at the mouth of the Blue Fish. They had moved the Elders and the youth earlier that day. No one got hurt, but there was damage done to the floor of our house. The flood lasted 40 minutes. It doesn't sound long, but it did do a lot of damage to houses.

Paul Josie
Chief Zzeh Gittlit School
Old Crow, Yukon

DND CANADA

Such was the case with unsung hero Gord Ives of Wheatley, Ontario. Located east of Leamington, Wheatley sustained a great deal of flood damage in 1998, and Gord's home was among the heaviest hit. Despite this, Gord allowed his neighbours to use his garage to store the lumber and other building materials that were donated by Toronto-based Green Forest Lumber. Gord even helped deliver the materials to the other victims, and made sure the needs of his neighbours were met before he was looked after. Every time we offered to help him, he insisted we look after the others first. His remarkable and generous spirit took him to the top of the volunteer effort, where he became its co-ordinator. By the time he focused attention on his own home, there was no lumber left for him.

In all, CVC solicited about $25,000 in labour and materials from construction suppliers, excavating companies, and local tradespeople. As well, we were able to rally support from a variety of sources — from corporations to government to the private sector. Buzz Hargrove, president of the Canadian Auto Workers, donated $10,000 on behalf of his union. CVC is grateful to Fairway Canadian Express Inc., of Toronto, Ontario who donated the use of their transport to deliver donated furniture and other essentials.

I stayed in touch with the families, and at the end of the year CVC decided to hold a large Christmas party for the children of families affected by the flood. Some families had suffered such financial loss that they worried they would not be able to give their children gifts that year. Although fire departments are wonderful in the way they help underprivileged children in communities across the country, CVC wanted to do something extra special in Essex County. Our organization's focus is always on adults, and sometimes we forget about the children in times of disaster. They experience extreme stress, too, but many times they suffer in silence. We solicited donations for toys and were able to bring some wonderful gifts and treats to these children and their parents.

In the same year, Lanark, a village in eastern Ontario, was threatened by flood waters. "Two hundred and fifty soldiers from CFB Petawawa responded to the call," said Second Lieutenant Luc Charron.

Volunteering
Is the way
To brighten up
A person's day.

Helping children in natural disasters
In Canada and overseas,
In your school
And communities.

It may not always be easy,
It may not always be fun,
But it's good to know
You've helped someone.

Lindsay Baldock
École W.S. Hawrylak School
Regina, Saskatchewan

COURTESY THE SALVATION ARMY

COURTESY OF *LEAMINGTON POST*

Looking over flooring estimates with flood victims Margaretha and Ben Dyck.

The definition of a volunteer is "someone who offers their own services at will." I hope that I can fulfill that description. You don't do these kind of things because you are forced to; you do them because you want to. It's a simple way to show others we care. Being a proud Canadian, I think volunteering is an important responsibility.

Casie Forster
École W.S. Hawrylak School
Regina, Saskatchewan

A year later, two more floods hit the province, one in the Ontario resort town of Huntsville, about 200 kilometres north of Toronto, the other just southeast of there in Haliburton/Burnt River.

DND CANADA

COURTESY, CONSTRUCTION VOLUNTEERS CANADA

With the owner of Lochlin Lumber, who assisted flood victims in Somerville.

With a family of flood victims, Mersea, Leamington, Ontario.

COURTESY, CONSTRUCTION VOLUNTEERS CANADA

A year later, two more floods hit the province, one in the Ontario resort town of Huntsville, about 200 kilometres north of Toronto, the other just southeast of there in Haliburton/Burnt River.

In Huntsville, CVC donated water. When I called the township with an offer of donated spring water, the official joked: "Well, I think we've got all the water we need." Many people don't realize that one of the things you lose in a flood — and one you can't afford to lose — is potable water.

In Haliburton/Burnt River, near the Ontario resort town of Haliburton, heavy rain and quick

Construction Volunteers Canada invited the Salvation Army to a Christmas party we hosted for Leamington flood victims.

COURTESY, CONSTRUCTION VOLUNTEERS CANADA

DND CANADA

A young girl stands on what is left of Highway 59 during the Manitoba flood. She's watching as a bulldozer from 2 Combat Engineer Regiment Petawawa clears a new route for the large gravel trucks to drop off sandbags along the waterline.

COURTESY THE *WINDSOR STAR*

Dressed as a clown for the Christmas party for child flood victims, Mersea, Leamington, Ontario, 1998.

melting snow caused water levels to surge. About 100 homes were damaged in the resulting flood. We worked to find donated construction materials to help out 18 victims — people who were most at risk — the elderly, the infirm, the physically challenged, and single parents.

The Canadian Tire Foundation for Families Helps Those in Need

On July, 3, 2000, Vanguard, Saskatchewan, experienced a 10-hour downpour that left the small town of 400 flooded under 33 centimetres of water. In response, the Canadian Tire Foundation for Families

THE WEATHER NETWORK

Driving through the flood waters.

COURTESY, CONSTRUCTION VOLUNTEERS CANADA

A tree uprooted during the Leamington floods.

COURTESY, CONSTRUCTION VOLUNTEERS CANADA

Assessing flood damage in Huntsville, Ontario, 1998.

10 Disasters That Struck London, Ontario

1. The Flood of July 1883. The north branch of the Thames River overflowed its banks in the early morning hours of July 11, 1883. Local resident James Dean was one of the first to realize the oncoming danger and rang the community bell to warn the town. Many were saved from serious disaster, but 18 people lost their lives. The electrical storm that occurred the same day destroyed the Imperial Oil Company refinery in what would later become East London.
2. The Electrical Storm of July 9–10, 1921. Lightning caused six fires in the city when 8 cm of rain fell within a 24-hour period, causing an estimated $750,000 in damage.
3. The Ice Storm of March 30, 1922. The storm caused thousands of dollars in damage to local trees.
4. The Flood of 1937. The Thames rose to the highest levels on record, causing $5 million in property damage and clean-up expenses. Dormitories were set up in the Armories, and the Canadian Red Cross set up a $100,000 emergency fund.
5. The Flood of April 5–6, 1947. Some 5,000 residents were evacuated as the north branch of the Thames crested within centimetres of the breakwater that had been heightened after the Flood of 1937. The main section of the river rose to within 67 cm of the 1937 level. A 78-year-old man refused to evacuate his home on Bathurst Street and drowned in only a foot of water in his own house.
6. The Ice Storm of 1968. The city suffered 32 mm of freezing rain in a little more than 12 hours. Some 30,000 homes were blacked out. Without electricity, people lined up, Depression-style, on January 15 outside the York Street premises of Dalton Fuels Ltd., to buy bags of coal.

7. The Blizzard of January 26, 1971. The city faced high winds, and 20.3 cm of snow fell, stopping schoolbuses from running, and leaving many children stranded at school. Some children were stranded at one school for three days.
8. The Ice Storm of March 2, 1976. The storm cost the city $175,000 in damages. More than 20,000 homes were without power. The staff at Jones Auto Body, which still had electricity, strung up a line of connected extension cords to the Cormier home on Third Street, enough to power two sump pumps, a hot plate, and the furnace — but only one appliance at a time.
9. Super Storm 1978. For 12 hours on January 26, 1978, some 32 cm of snow dumped on the city, and winds reached 128 km/h, knocking down signs and blowing out windows in the downtown area. Boris Melynyk, the manager of the Woolworth store on Dundas Street, made it to work, but most of his employees did not. Unable to return home, he opened the store, fired up the snack bar, and offered warm drinks and light snacks to anybody who came along.
10. The Tornado of September 2, 1984. At about 7:30 p.m. on a quiet Sunday, a tornado touched down in London, hitting the White Oaks and Cleardale subdivisions the hardest. The tornado caused $5 million in damage to 600 houses and 50 businesses, and injured 30 people. Fortunately, there were no fatalities. Diane Morrison of Cleardale bought groceries for the unfortunate residents of a demolished townhouse two blocks away. The food was distributed by the Salvation Army.

— Dan Brock
History teacher
Catholic Central High School
London, Ontario

In the flood of 1937, the waters of the Thames (London, Ontario) rose 7 metres. I was an 11-year-old Boy Scout. The two branches of the river were flooded as a result of heavy spring rains and melting snow. The Fanshawe dam was yet to be built, and the water easily spilled over the breakwaters built to contain it. The waters rose slowly, giving people time to escape and head for higher ground. The Armories was a popular refuge where I handed out blankets to people taking shelter. Finally, my turn was done, and I headed home, but they wouldn't let me cross Ridout Bridge — the waters were too high and had already covered the top of the bridge. I went back to the Armories, where I was stranded for two days. Four days later the waters finally receded. There was one fatality: a policeman, who had jumped out of his boat and stepped into an open manhole. He couldn't find his way out, and drowned.

Frank Fitzmaurice
interviewed by Mallory Carpenter &
Amy O'Neill
St. Martin Catholic School
London, Ontario

COURTESY, CONSTRUCTION VOLUNTEERS CANADA

With a flood victim and a load of donated lumber from Toronto, in Mersea-Leamington, 1998.

CHAPTER 4

The Pine Lake Tornado

July 14, 2000

DIANE LEWIS, RED DEER COUNTY

RED DEER, ALBERTA/DELBURNE CENTRALIZED SCHOOL, DELBURNE, ALBERTA

The aftermath of the Pine Lake tornado.

FOR THE RECORD

- 12 were killed, more than 140 injured
- the tornado travelled for 15 to 20 km at a speed of more than 300 km/h
- $10,000 in donations was raised by the Canadian Red Cross
- 2.8 million kilograms of debris was hauled from the site
- $9.5 million was spent by Alberta and federal governments on recovery programs: $4 million to victims; $5.5 million for rescue and clean-up

TAKE A SEVERE THUNDERSTORM, ADD A BAND OF LOW-LEVEL MOISTURE AND YOU have a recipe for mass destruction. Such was the lethal cocktail that roared in off the foothills of the Rocky Mountains on Friday, July 14, 2000, travelled northeast across the plains, and touched down 5 kilometres west of the Green Acres campground in Pine Lake, Alberta, at about 7 p.m., as hundreds of vacationing families were finishing dinner. The beautiful summer day had began as a perfect prelude to a hot, clear weekend. There was no advance warning of a tornado; weather updates had called for thunderstorms. And since the campground is situated in a valley surrounded by hills, it was impossible for the campers to have a visual cue that a tornado was barrelling towards them.

COURTESY RCMP

Destruction at Pine Lake.

NATIONAL ARCHIVES OF CANADA/C33275

Cyclone damage in Regina, Saskatchewan, 1912.

Anatomy of a Disaster: The Pine Lake Tornado

For the many campers at Green Acres Campground at Pine Lake, there was no better way to spend a summer evening than relaxing at the trailer. The severe thunderstorm watch at 5:37 p.m. on the evening of Friday, July 14, 2000, must have seemed only a minor setback. Half an hour later, the watch was upgraded to a storm warning, which meant that a severe storm was a near certainty. Yet, by the time it was reported at 7:05 p.m., the fourth-worst tornado in Canadian history was already devastating Pine Lake.

One of the most frustrating aspects of tornadoes is how impossible they are to predict. Scientists know that warm humid weather travelling north from the Gulf of Mexico and colliding with a cool front can produce severe thunderstorms, which can result in tornadoes. The thunderstorm that produced the Pine Lake tornado started in the foothills of Alberta and travelled east. When its path crossed a narrow band of low-level moisture, it developed into a severe thunderstorm with heavy rain, lightning, large hail, and dangerous winds. While scientists know that updrafts and downdrafts play a role in causing rotation within storm clouds, they still don't know why clouds within some storms rotate and those in others don't, or why some rotations develop into tornadoes while others don't. They do know that most tornadoes emerge from storms in the peak season of May to September, and that tornadoes tend to strike along specific "corridors," one of which is in Alberta. High-tech Doppler radar can measure wind and rain patterns associated with a tornado, but an eyewitness account still remains the most reliable way of spotting one.

Canada is hit by about 80 tornadoes a year, but few are fatal. The last tornado in Canada to cause loss of human life was the Edmonton tornado of 1987, which left 27 dead and hundreds injured. That tornado rated an F4 on the Fujita scale, compared to the Pine Lake tornado's rating of F3. (The Fujita scale, which is the tornado equivalent of the Richter scale, classifies tornadoes from F0 to F5 in intensity, with F5 being the most destructive.) The average tornado follows a path about 100 metres wide and 2 kilometres long and has a core wind speed of less than 160 km/hour. The tornado that struck Pine Lake travelled a path between 800 and 1,500 metres wide and 15 to 20 kilometres long. From the damage to the region, experts estimate that wind speed in its 500-metre central corridor was 300 km/hour.

By 8:00 p.m. that evening, the tornado had passed Green Acres, but the destruction remained. Of the 140 people injured, 12 died from their injuries. The damage to the campground and the surrounding farms amounted to more than $10 million, but the damage to lives was immeasurable.

Twelve people were killed,
Their bodies ever stilled.
Southern Ontario's tornadoes are
usually weak, they say,
But not this one that struck Barrie
in the month of May.
It's amazing what Mother Nature
is capable of
Taking away friends and the ones
we love.

Kortnie Foll, Jessica Sauve,
Amanda Sutherland, Ami Arsenault,
Lindsay Bernier, Amanda Damas
The Good Shepherd Catholic School
Barrie, Ontario

The Barrie, Ontario, Tornado Left Hundreds Homeless

When a tornado ripped through Barrie, Grand Valley, and Tecumseth Township on May 31, 1985, it left 12 dead, and hundreds homeless, and caused millions of dollars in damage.

The storm, which began in the late afternoon, touched down first in Barrie. A few minutes later, another tornado came down just north of Arthur and remained on the ground for 90 km as it tracked east-northeast at 85 km/h to the Holland Marsh. It then skipped along a further 17 km before lifting off permanently.

The width of the damage path was typically between 150 and 400 metres but at some points jumped to 600 metres. Nearly all structures within this track were damaged.

From Arthur to Grand Valley, the damage path ranged from 150 to 400 metres wide. Tornado winds were estimated to exceed 400 km/h. About 40 buildings were seriously damaged or destroyed along the way. In Grand Valley itself, 101 homes near the centre of the tornado track were destroyed. Two hundred other buildings on the edge of the track suffered varying degrees of damage. The library roof was lifted and thrown 200 metres before crashing down on a house. In one town, two people were killed, one a visitor from Scotland.

From east of Grand Valley to Orangeville, the path of destruction continued 150 to 300 metres wide. Mono Plaza, north of Orangeville, was levelled, but miraculously no one was killed. Particularly hard hit was the area just south of Tottenham, where about 15 homes were extensively damaged or levelled and two deaths were reported. Tree damage and some property damage was reported along the track of the second swath.

The tornado moved down into the Holland Marsh just southeast of Dunkerron and followed the canal road eastward and then northeastward for about 5 km. It destroyed hundreds of trees along the canal and did considerable damage to buildings along the north canal road. The tornado then headed directly east toward the marsh, hitting the village of Ansnorveldt after destroying three hydro transmission towers.

East of Holland Marsh, the storm began skipping, causing less serious, intermittent damage. It finally lifted off near Mount Albert.

Officers working on the disaster put in 12- to 14-hour days. Local citizens took in tornado victims by the hundreds.

— from the *OPP Review*,
October 1985

It starts off with a little breeze.
The sky begins to darken.
Everyone runs and hides
From the terrible winds that lurk outside.

Eric Medeiros, Ascension of Our Lord School,
Mississauga, Ontario

DIANE LEWIS, RED DEER COUNTY

Ground zero at Pine Lake.

THE WEATHER NETWORK

The remains of a child's bedroom that was demolished by a 1996 tornado in Arthur, Ontario.

About 30 minutes later, it was all over, and 12 people lay dead. The tornado cut a swath through the grounds measuring between 800 and 1,500 metres wide. The winds of more than 300 kilometres per hour and hailstones the size of baseballs left little remaining that was recognizable. In addition to the destruction of 400 campsites, dozens of nearby farms and fields were severely damaged.

"If you saw the movie *Twister*, that's about what it was like," said one Pine Lake survivor.

The sight of bloodied, panic-stricken, and dazed faces, uprooted trees, flattened homes and cars, and shredded trailers is etched on the minds of the Pine Lake survivors, save for those like Phyllis Gallenberg, who is glad to have no memory of the event. The then 74-year-old resident of Stettler, Alberta, was sucked out of her car by the tornado and thrown across the campground. Rescuers found her battered and bleeding body and, assuming she was dead, covered her up and left her. When a campground employee walked past her and heard a faint cry, Ms. Gallenberg was airlifted to hospital. She lost a leg and an elbow, and skin grafts were used to patch a large hole above her eyebrow. "All my friends from the lake have visited me and told me about [the

---

The deadliest tornado ever recorded in Canada was the Regina cyclone of 1912. It killed 40 people and injured 300. It also damaged 500 buildings. If I was around during that time, I surely would have helped the people by donating my time to fundraise in order to cover the costs of the damages. If I was in their place, I would have written a letter to the Prime Minister of Canada requesting temporary shelter for the innocent people whose houses were destroyed before their eyes.

Shazaad Khan
Morning Star Middle School
Mississauga, Ontario

tornado]," Ms. Gallenberg told a reporter for the Canadian Press. "I think it's good that I don't remember."

What people do remember are the hundreds and hundreds of people who descended on Pine Lake within minutes of the disaster to tend to the survivors and retrieve the remains of the 12 people who had lost their lives.

RCMP Staff-Sergeant Warren Forsythe was one of the first on the scene and described an eerie calm. "It looked like a war zone," remembers Forsythe. "We expected hysteria, but people were in shock. There was nothing you could do to prepare for this," Sgt. Forsythe said, in an article published in the RCMP's newsmagazine *Pony Express*. "The initial response was huge; the fire department, municipal police, ambulances, even people from the campsite were carrying stretchers and transporting injured people in their own pick-up trucks. It was a real joint effort."

Among the heroes, according to Sgt. Forsythe, were the telecommunications officers who managed calls from distressed relatives and local and international media, and co-ordinated the hundreds of offers from community members to donate food, clothing, and equipment. Among these operators were Radio Amateur of Canada members, a little-known group of 34,000 radio operators. According to Pierre Mainville, its vice-president of field services, RAC alerts and mobilizes volunteer communications personnel and equipment, and sets up and maintains fixed, mobile, and portable links to allow emergency agencies to communicate with various locations.

More than 1,600 volunteers, including trained members from 24 search-and-rescue units, provided disaster relief services. The Canadian Red Cross registered an astounding 1,100 people, who travelled to Pine Lake, about 60 kilometres southeast of Red Deer, to offer help.

Six aircraft companies, eight ambulance attendant organizations, and two dispatch organizations were involved in getting the seriously injured transported to regional hospitals. The Civil Air Search and Rescue Association (CASARA), a Canada-wide volunteer aviation association, set up a temporary morgue and provided coffee and food for the pilots and medical personnel. CASARA also mapped the tornado track the following morning and searched the outlying areas

The tornado has made the children in my class hypersensitive to weather conditions. On a number of occasions, a few of them have been brought to tears by their fear.

Gabrielle Lamb
(teacher)
Delburne Centralized School
Delburne, Alberta

There were three little boys who were walking home from their friend's house and suddenly it began to rain hard. One little boy wanted to keep walking, while the other two went back to their friend's house. The one little boy did not make it home. The tornado picked him up and later his body was found on the railway tracks.

Anne Foll, Barrie resident, as told to Kortnie Foll, Jessica Sauve, Amanda Sutherland, Ami Arsenault, Lindsay Bernier
The Good Shepherd Catholic School
Barrie, Ontario

In July, 1996, in Port Perry, Ontario, I was visiting my grandparents. In the night, my mom woke up my brother Mark and me. "Get up, and go to the basement," she said. My mom went into my grandparents' room and woke them up and told them she thought she heard a train going over the house. The sound had been made by tornadoes! Three tornadoes were close to the house. They had formed on Lake Scugog, which is about 100 feet away from my grandparents' house. We ran downstairs and my parents wrapped Mark and me in a blanket. The tornadoes were destructive and travelled on through Port Perry to Lindsay. About half an hour later, it was all over. We looked through the window. Five trees were destroyed and a chunk from my grandparents' garage was gone. It was an extremely scary experience.

Megan Gilmour and Sarah Brooks
Byron Northview Public School
London, Ontario

for victims. The City of Calgary Fire Department and Calgary Emergency Medical Services dispatched 23 emergency personnel and 11 vehicles to the site. Sailors from the Navy's Maritime Pacific Command in Esquimalt, British Columbia, arrived with high-resolution sonar devices to map the bottom of Pine Lake. "Four sailors from the Acoustic Data Analysis Centre used high-resolution side-scan sonar to map objects on the bottom of Pine Lake," said Navy Lieutenant Mike Brissette.

It seemed every town and city in the area immediately came forth with offers of assistance and comfort for the survivors. Businesses also chipped in. The night the tornado hit, Joe Dand, the owner of the local Canadian Tire, opened his store to rescue workers, telling them to take what they needed, which included chainsaws, rain suits, oil, and gas. Wal-Mart contributed clothing and cots. Rubbermaid donated 1,200 storage containers so campers could salvage their belongings. Community members brought sandwiches and took in survivors whose homes had been destroyed. The Knights of Columbus set up a relief fund. Construction Volunteers Canada sent donations to Red Deer County officials.

COURTESY RCMP

Pine Lake destruction.

"What came out of this," says Sgt. Forsythe, "was that it showed all of us this huge outpouring of public support. Their generosity of time and compassion restored my faith after 28 years of dealing with the other side of human nature."

Watching all of this from a frighteningly close vantage point was Josh Stegman, a teenager from Red Deer who had been vacationing with his family that day at Pine Lake. After the tornado hit, Josh lay bruised and bleeding. He had no idea where the rest of his family was, or whether they were hurt. The injured were quickly assessed and dispatched to different hospitals according to the severity of their condition. Josh had suffered major injuries and was hospitalized for two-and-a-half months. His mother and grandmother each spent two months in hospital. It was days before Josh learned that his father was among those killed during the tornado's fury — no one had the heart to tell him. Josh was in intensive care, clinging to life. His mother and grandmother were at different hospitals.

COURTESY THE WEATHER NETWORK

A mother looks over what's left of her tornado-ravaged home in Arthur, Ontario, in 1996.

A big wind is coming.
The Niagara Peninsula Tornado of 1898
A kilometre wide, to destroy was its task.
When would it give up? No one had a clue.
People's lives were in danger
And there was nothing they could do.
So people die, people are hurt.
They all had to deal with the loss.
Just one more time Mother Nature proved she was boss.

Annalice Hill
Canadian Martyrs Catholic School
Oshawa, Ontario

COURTESY THE WEATHER NETWORK

A cradle remains standing in a home destroyed by the Arthur, Ontario, tornado of 1996.

It was July 8, 1995, and Emily and her family were enjoying their holidays at their cottage in Bridgenorth on Chemong Lake (near Peterborough, Ontario). The peaceful night was interrupted by the sound of thunder and a flash of lightning. Emily and her parents suddenly woke up and rushed around, closing windows, gathering swimsuits off the clothesline, and folding up the outdoor furniture. Satisfied that the cottage was ready for the winds and rain, Emily's parents settled inside to watch. They watched lawn ornaments and furniture flying through the air. A garbage pail sailed by the beach. Shingles were torn from the boathouse, and debris from other cottages flew by. Emily could feel the tension of her parents, but they did not say a word. Instead, they held her close. They slowly moved away from the huge window, trying not to seem worried. The wind howled, and pieces of the cottage were being pulled from the shell; eavestrough, loose shingles, and shutters were freed by the strong winds. Despite the damage of the terrible tornado that hit the village, not one person died. The community and the volunteers from Peterborough banded together to help others and to restore order in the area.

Lacey Baldwin
King Edward Public School
Peterborough, Ontario

PINE LAKE TORNADO 2000

That night, I thought everything was chaotic, but to my surprise I found out that it was really handled so professionally and was so organized. There are so many people that I classify as heroes to my family, it would be impossible to name them all. From the people who helped me at the site, to the wonderful people who came to visit me and continue to help my family, I have learned so much.

When a disaster strikes, no matter how big or how many people are hurt, it is absolutely necessary that there are people trained to deal with a disaster. It is because of these people that the death toll at Pine Lake was not higher. It was a terrifying feeling that complete strangers made all major decisions for me in seconds.

They say there are more and more tornadoes every year. Maybe we have always had tornadoes but they would just rip through a farmer's field. We thought that was the end of it. [But] central Alberta's population is growing fast. There is less and less open space; it makes us a bigger target.

When people in general go camping, it is to get away from the big city. Campers do not have television and radios turned on. There needs to be a new warning system and guidelines for campgrounds so we can prevent tragedies like Pine Lake. Central Alberta should have a meteorologist that is right there in our region, not in Edmonton or Calgary. Meteorologists in these places have no idea what the weather is like 200 kilometres away in Red Deer [where weather patterns are different]. We should not be satisfied with long-distance monitoring. Right now, the maximum alert time is between 10 and 20 minutes. How are you supposed to get out of the path or be prepared for a tornado in 10 minutes?

— Josh Stegman
Red Deer, Alberta

In the summer of 1998, a lightning bolt hit a tree and it came crashing down. As we were driving off the highway, I saw a funnel cloud forming. I told my mom that this felt like a nightmare. When I got home, my whole family went down to the basement. As the tornado passed, I heard a terrifying whistle. Five minutes later, the tornado was gone and the sky was blue. The fence was destroyed, and some of the branches on our tree were thrown to the other side of the street.

Patrick McCarthy
Hadley Junior High School
Hull, Quebec

A family who was in a tornado moved to Nova Scotia. They had a three-month-old girl. When they came to Halifax they had nothing. Father announced during Mass what had happened to the family. That day, some of the people in the church brought food, beds, diapers, blankets, toys, TV, VCR, movies, shoes, outerwear, and telephones. One week later, the family called to say thank you.

Allysyn Walsh
Fairview Heights Elementary School
Halifax, Nova Scotia

THE WEATHER NETWORK

After the Arthur, Ontario, tornado.

One night in Alexandria, Ontario, in 1999, my cousin and I went to sleep in our tent. It was about 11 p.m. I fell asleep, but then I suddenly woke up listening to the high winds and the sound of the pins hitting the tent. The tent's ceiling fell down and we were hurled into the cornfield at a tremendous speed, still inside the tent. I was trying to zip down the zipper to get us out but I got my leg stuck between the middle poles and it was cutting my leg. My cousin got the zipper open and got us out. The winds were incredible; I could hardly stay on my feet. I wondered how a wind like that could pick up a tent that was nailed to the ground, two people, and two mattresses. We were lost in the cornfield, but we finally found a road. We walked and finally got back to the house. My aunt was looking around and saw us and she looked like she had been crying. She was really worried about us and gave us huge hugs, and she brought us back into the house where she made us some hot chocolate.

Colin Sauve
Hadley Junior High School
Hull, Quebec

Josh's mother, Lynn, marvels to this day at Josh's recovery.

"They never expected Josh to walk again," she says. "But he walks fine. He is starting back into sports. He is my inspiration. Everyday he teaches me to turn fear into hope, and pain into compassion."

Josh is a remarkable person, a survivor. Most children who survived the disaster, however, especially younger children, suffer recurring nightmares and phobias because of their experience at Pine Lake. For some, the sight of a mere leaf rustling reminds them that a gentle breeze can suddenly morph into a terrifying and deadly wind.

Red Deer County documented some of these fears after speaking with children who were at the campground: "I saw my brother thrown to the ground as he tried to get from a trailer to the house"; "Trees and buildings started to fall, and I started to pray"; "My parents weren't home, and I didn't know who would protect me, but I also didn't know if my parents would be safe"; "I got sick to my stomach when the wind started rocking the trailer."

Gabrielle Lamb, a Grade Two teacher at Delburne Centralized School in Delburne, Alberta, saw fear in her own classroom: "The tornado has made the children in my class hypersensitive to weather conditions. Indeed, on a number of occasions, a few of them have been brought to tears by their fear." She took action — she requested the children receive training from the Canadian Red Cross on Personal Disaster Preparedness, and she organized a meeting to encourage other elementary teachers to do the same. "The program was beneficial in alleviating [the children's] distress," she later wrote to me. "It was helpful to me, also, because I can now answer their questions with more knowledge." The Canadian Red Cross, in conjunction with Chinook's Edge School Division, initiated an emergency preparedness program, which will become part of the curriculum in the region.

More than 40 tornadoes materialize each year on the Canadian prairies, 16 of them in Alberta. Canada ranks second in the world for tornado activity, behind the United States.

The first recorded tornado in Canadian history occurred on June 30, 1792, in Ontario's Niagara Peninsula between the towns of Fonthill and Port Robinson. It levelled homes and cleared a wide path through the woods between two villages. Hurricane Road was later built along this path.

On August 1, 1995, in Paltimore, Quebec, it began raining and thundering, and my two brothers and my dad were outside putting round bales of hay away in the shed before they got wet. The wind was fierce. Before they realized the danger they were in, the hay-shed roof took off like a kite. The beams were falling in the barn and my brothers and dad were hiding behind the gravity box for safety. They couldn't believe what was happening. They looked at the roof flying in the air and realized they had no choice: They ran for the house. When the storm finally went by, we went outside to see the mess. The hay bales were out under the blue sky lying everywhere, the oats in the gravity box were wet. There was a big beam that had fallen on the end of the gravity box, about 6 inches from where my dad and brothers had hidden. People driving by and neighbours came to see what happened. The news reporter was called and came. Nobody could believe no one had been hurt.

Tiffany Adam
Hadley Junior High School
Hull, Quebec

There have been other deadly tornadoes in Canada. On May 31, 1985, 12 people were killed, 155 injured, and farms and livestock were destroyed in Barrie, Ontario. Metropolitan Toronto Police Auxiliaries responded, helping to secure the disaster area while citizens gathered their belongings and tried to rebuild their shattered lives. On July 31, 1987, one of the worst tornadoes in Canadian history swept through Edmonton, killing 27 and injuring 300. In both events, volunteers provided prompt and critical help.

CHAPTER 5

The Salmon Arm Forest Fire

July 29, 1998

ONTARIO MINISTRY OF NATURAL RESOURCES

Every year thousands of hectares of forests are destroyed by forest fires that could have been prevented.

FOR THE RECORD

- 8,000 people fled their homes
- 6,500 hectares were burned
- 40 buildings and 16 homes were destroyed
- $10 million was spent to extinguish the fire

One day in the summer of 1997, my mother, Anastasia Qupee, was on her way home from Goose Bay. On the way, she noticed smoke in the forest near Gosling Park. She was stopped by police and was told she could not get through because the smoke was too thick. My mom had to go back to Goose Bay because the road was closed. She returned and saw firemen putting out the fire. She was very tired and happy to be home with her family.

Jonathan Andrew
Peenamin McKenzie School,
Sheshatshiu, Labrador

THOSE OF US WHO LIVE IN THE CITY CAN'T BEGIN TO COMPREHEND THE AMOUNT OF land that is swallowed up each year by forest fires in this country, the devastation they cause, or the speed at which they spread. Their frequency and sheer size have always amazed me. Human carelessness is responsible for 58 percent of all forest fires; the rest is caused by lightning.

Forest fires are not necessarily bad things. They are, in fact, vital for the regeneration of grassland and reforestation. Some species actually depend on fires to reproduce. For instance, certain types of pine trees produce resin-sealed cones that stay on the trees for years. The heat from the fire melts the resin and the cones pop open, releasing thousands of seeds that grow into new stands of pine. Even plants and animals depend on fire to open up areas that weren't accessible to them, or to expose certain insects, like bark beetles, to the hungry mouths of birds.

So fire can be a good thing. But try telling that to people whose homes are mere kilometres from the scene of a forest fire.

ONTARIO MINISTRY OF NATURAL RESOURCES

Once the fire has burnt over a piece of land, the tedious mop-up begins. Here, Ontario Ranger crews scour every inch of the burn looking for hotspots.

Anatomy of a Disaster: The Salmon Arm Forest Fire

On Monday August 13, 1998, 7,000 residents of Salmon Arm, British Columbia, were given 10 minutes to evacuate their homes. The forest fire that had been stalemating firefighters for two weeks was in danger of burning out of control yet again. This was the second time that this blaze had driven people from their homes: The residents of Silver Creek had been evacuated the week before when strong winds drove the fire past the emergency barriers and towards their village at 100 metres a minute. It was these winds, combined with the dry forest, that had spread this fire across 63 square kilometres.

While there is disagreement over whether El Niño was a factor, there can be no denying that it was a hot and dry year. Many claim that 1998 was one of the worst forest fire seasons in Canadian history, with 10,560 forest fires across Canada destroying 4.6 million hectares of forests — about 50 percent more than the normal amount. Of all provinces, however, British Columbia was the hardest hit. That summer the province spent more than $50 million fighting forest fires; $55,000 a day of that was pitted against the fire that raged around Salmon Arm.

Pine forests are a common fire risk in the summer, and an early spring combined with unusually high temperatures (daytime temperatures averaged 30° C) made for dry and volatile conditions that summer around Salmon Arm. After 17 days without rain, lightning started a forest fire near the town, on July 29, 1998. Winds reaching 60 km/hour spread the fire through the tinder-dry forests and turned a 0.1-hectare fire into a 10-hectare blaze within two hours. The remote location of the blaze made it difficult for firefighters to bring in the necessary equipment, and, as the dry days continued, it was clear that the rain was not going to come. If anything, the weather was their biggest opponent; recurring strong winds inflamed hot spots and spread the fire out of control. It would take 21 days of constant fire fighting and emergency measures to get the fire under control, and even then it continued to burn.

Some people debated whether the government had done enough to prevent the worst of the damages, arguing that the fire should never have been allowed to burn out of control in the first place. However, fire crews were on the scene from the beginning, with a dozen water bombers in use every day. Though the town remained on alert, residents were allowed to return to their homes within a week. Before the blaze was brought under control, however, 40 residences were destroyed, and many people's lives were thrown into chaos.

ONTARIO MINISTRY OF NATURAL RESOURCES

In 1999, a 50,000-hectare forest fire burned to the doorstep of the northern town of Beardmore, Ontario. The fire, known as Nip 12, was started by a careless resident burning debris.

The worst fire in recent history occurred in Manitoba, where fires in 1989 burned 3.5 million hectares, and forced 24,000 people out of their homes in 32 communities. About 100 homes were destroyed.

In 1998, Salmon Arm, British Columbia, a mountain community of about 15,000 located 400 kilometres northeast of Vancouver, faced the flames in what began as a typical forest fire.

In the afternoon of July 29, lightning hit a tree in the Fly Hills, about 20 kilometres away from the town. Fueled by dry heat and wind, the fire quickly developed a voracious appetite and was, by Day 3, consuming its 40th hectare of forest. By Day 7, the fire's devastation had ballooned to 3,000 hectares, then doubled itself seven days later. By the time the fire was brought under control, 6,300 hectares had been incinerated.

THE WEATHER NETWORK

The Salmon Arm, British Columbia, forest fire, 1998.

Back in 1985 and 1991, there were forest fires started by thunder and lightning storms. In 1985, people from Sheshatshiu and nearby Northwest River were sent to Goose Bay. On a hot summer day on July 10, 1997, three people started a forest fire in Kenamesh by accident. The people involved said they just wanted to make the grass grow, so they started a small fire. The fire spread over the whole island. A water bomber put out the fire, but not before many cabins and tents burned down.

Ann Philomena Hurley
Peenamin McKenzie School
Sheshatshiu, Labrador

ONTARIO MINISTRY OF NATURAL RESOURCES

Wetting the underbrush at Obatanga Provincial Park, 2001.

ONTARIO MINISTRY OF NATURAL RESOURCES

The Mennonites promptly responded to Salmon Arm's SOS. They quickly set up a full-service disaster centre that included an emergency co-ordination centre and a command post.

Although Construction Volunteers Canada did not get involved in the fire, I called the municipality to offer construction materials and to see whether there was someone directly affected by the fire with whom I could speak and offer words of comfort and encouragement. I was given the name of an elderly gentleman, Walter Mott. When I called Mr. Mott he was as consumed with grief as anyone can be who is about to lose everything he owned. He had been hosing down his roof, trying to save it from the heat and flames that threatened to ignite it.

Mr. Mott, who was in his 80s, told me how he had cleared the land as a young man, built a home and raised his family. He had spent his life farming the area. Now it was all about to be destroyed; he was distraught.

It is difficult to talk to a stranger who pours out his life story to you. You feel helpless, yet in a way, you're all that person has at that moment. I asked him to think back to when he first cleared the land, the back-breaking work he had done and how the sense of satisfaction and accomplishment had spurred him on. "How many people do that?" I asked him. Hadn't the lesson of self-sufficiency been something he wanted to pass on to his children? What would they think if he gave up now?

I think my lecture worked: He decided that if he lost his house, he and his son would simply rebuild it. The fire had not eradicated his entrepreneurial spirit.

THE WEATHER NETWORK

In the spring of 1989, our family was living in a tent in the country near a place called Mininipi. The tents were put up on caribou moss and evergreen boughs. All the men, except my uncle, had gone hunting. My aunt was behind my grandmother's tent when she heard a strange, unfamiliar sound. Looking into the woods, she saw the forest was on fire, and it was coming quickly toward the tent! She screamed, and everyone ran outside. My mother called out to my brother and sister, who were playing on a swing beside our tent. She told my sister to take my brother and me down to the edge of the lake. My grandmother's tent caught fire, and within a few moments it had burned up, along with everything inside. My mother and uncle kept our tent from burning by using water that they gathered from the lake in our buckets. My mother tells me she will never forget how quickly the fire raced up the trees from the burning moss on the ground.

Penute Andrew

Peenamin McKenzie School

Sheshatshiu, Labrador

THE WEATHER NETWORK

ONTARIO MINISTRY OF NATURAL RESOURCES

Checking the hoses in northwestern Ontario, 2001.

The Yellowknife fire of 1997 was started by a thunderstorm. It filled the town's sky with ash and turned it dark grey. The Prelude and Reid lake areas were evacuated. People lost their homes or cabins and their valuables. Pets were killed. It took days to get the fire under control. People who had cabins where the fire was headed were brought to their homes by helicopter to gather some belongings before the fire destroyed everything. The fire left an endless trail of burned trees, household items, and dead animals. Cabin owners were left in shock and disbelief.

Samantha Digness
Range Lake North School,
Yellowknife, Northwest Territories

During the firestorm of 2003, I saw the fire from my roof. I saw a tree candling – I saw water bombers and I saw the Mars Bomber. I saw helicopters, and smoke everywhere. We started packing!

Alanna Jo Tulman
Ecole Belgo Elementary School
Kelowna, British Columbia

Tree Canada Foundation provides support to communities affected by natural disasters. Assistance was provided to the Saguenay flood, and Icestorm in Eastern/Western Quebec. We look forward to helping communities in central B.C. who were affected by the wildfires of 2003.

Jeff Monty
Tree Canada Foundation

It was the same can-do spirit that spurred friends and strangers into action.

Brenda Toews, a member of the Church of God and Christ Mennonite from nearby Enderby, arrived to see if she could help. She was handed a key to the Salvation Army Food Bank and spent the next several days directing the enormous task of feeding the firefighters. On the first night, she and her crew prepared 2,000 sandwiches.

Silver Creek resident Wendy Howes worried for the safety of her neighbour's horses during the evacuation. She didn't have time to load them onto her truck; instead she threw a saddle on one and led the rest of the herd to safety.

Barb Brouwer, a resident of Salmon Arm, tells how the small community made it through on its own strength and with the help of treasured volunteers.

"Over the course of 15 days, literally thousands of volunteers worked tirelessly to support and feed firefighters and Emergency Operations Centre staff, provide information to worried residents, and open their homes to people and animals displaced by the fire. Volunteers flocked to the EOC to maintain emergency phone lines set

ONTARIO MINISTRY OF NATURAL RESOURCES

The CL-415 Ontario Water Bomber in action.

COURTESY FOREST INDUSTRIES FLYING TANKERS LTD.

The mighty Martin Mars flying tanker, perfectly suited for fighting fires in British Columbia's coastal forests.

ONTARIO MINISTRY OF NATURAL RESOURCES

Ontario Ranger crews have an exciting but dangerous job, often working at the edge of a fire. During an intense fire such as this one, the crews are supported from the air by helicopters and heavy water bombers.

up for the public. Finding people to keep these phone lines open 24 hours a day was never a problem. In fact, more people volunteered than could be accepted. Volunteers from the Salvation Army, Emergency Social Services, Shuswap Emergency Preparedness, and the Society for the Prevention of Cruelty to Animals donated their time and talents to help evacuate and keep track of people and their animals."

The help did not end when the fire was put out. In the fall, volunteers returned to Salmon Arm to clear debris and help people rebuild their homes. Under the co-ordination of former Silver Creek resident Fimmy Ganshorn, more than $210,000 was raised for homebuilding projects. The Mennonite community helped 10 families rebuild their homes and outbuildings.

As with all fires, the firefighters are the hands-down heroes.

Every year, provincial governments and Parks Canada hire and train hundreds of firefighters, creating an industry that comes alive for six months of the year. These men and women work under hard, hot, exhausting conditions. Take an average summer day, add 1,000 degrees and extremely dangerous conditions, and you get an idea of what their work must be like. After they extinguish one blaze, they are airlifted out and transported to a new fire in another province, where they serve as reinforcements for a cadre of firefighters already worn down by a blaze that is out of control.

In addition to the ground forces, forest fires are fought with a battalion of helicopters, rappel crews, water tankers, and even satellite monitoring systems. Martin Mars water bombers, reputed to be the largest in the world, were conscripted for the Salmon Arm fire.

More than 2,000 civilian firefighters worked on this particular fire. They were assisted by about 100 soldiers, among them Charlie Company of the 3rd Battalion, Princess Patricia's Canadian Light Infantry Regiment from Calgary, who had fought fires in Alberta and New Brunswick. A year earlier, the regiment had helped out in the Manitoba flood.

D'Arcy McLeod, a resident of Salmon Arm, wrote a diary of the tense, terrifying days when his town was under siege:

COURTESY CANADIAN AIR-CRANE LTD.

Skycranes accurately deliver a high volume of water or flame retardant to a forest fire site, quickly suppressing the fire and saving lives.

Emergency Management Ontario Provides Shelter

Ontario faced a difficult forest fire season in 1995. In June of that year, Emergency Management Ontario (EMO) set up three evacuation centres to accommodate 420 residents from Wunnumin Lake and 630 residents from Kasabonika (Geraldon Evacuation Centre); 192 residents of Deer Lake and 103 from Sachigo Lake (Thunder Bay Evacuation Centre); and 66 residents from Kee-Way-Win and Couchiching and 177 from Muskrat Dam (Red Lake Evacuation Centre). EMO provided materials for arts and crafts as well as games to help children deal with the separation from their homes and communities. Some of the children's parents stayed at home to help fight the forest fires, which stressed the children as well.

— Emergency Management Ontario

ONTARIO MINISTRY OF NATURAL RESOURCES

Obatanga Provincial Park, 2001.

ONTARIO MINISTRY OF NATURAL RESOURCES

Obatanga Provincial Park, 2001, as a plane flies overhead.

CERV

The Community Emergency Response Volunteers Ontario (CERV) program was announced Sept. 10, 2002 as part of the Ontario government's on-going commitment to improving emergency response and management. CERV is a province-wide grass-roots network of teams of volunteers trained in basic emergency management principles and skills. Ontario's retirees, especially retired police officers, firefighters and paramedics will be targeted for recruitment. These volunteers will use their experience and expertise to liaise with current emergency front-line responders. Criteria for membership and training will be co-ordinated through Emergency Management Ontario, with municipal emergency management co-ordinators organizing training in their jurisdictions. Volunteers will be trained in basic emergency skills, disaster response and light search and rescue operations.

— Emergency Management Ontario

After returning from a camping trip 300 km to the north, we arrive at the city limits at about 10:30 p.m. It is like driving into hell. There is blowing smoke and ash with very strong wind gusts. I sense chaos and panic. There are cars and people everywhere, and the smell of burning timber fills the air. Driving into town, my wife gasps when she sees that the side of Mount Ida is on fire.

Forty structures and 16 homes were destroyed in Silver Creek today. Hundreds of people were evacuated from their homes. The fire crossed the valley floor (agricultural fields and a river) and raced up the side of Ida in minutes. The fire was clocked moving at a rate of 100 metres a minute. Parts of the town have been put on evacuation alert. The fire is now listed at 550 hectares, but everyone knows it is bigger. The smoke is so thick the B.C. Ministry of Forests cannot accurately measure the size of the burn.

ONTARIO MINISTRY OF NATURAL RESOURCES

Making a backyard stand, Terrace Bay, 1985.

The lightning that struck the mountain and started the fire occurred on July 29, 1998, and became a firestorm on August 5, 1998. It looked like an atomic bomb had gone off. The Fly Hills, where we live, were in flames. My mom dropped us off at our grandma's place and took off right away for our house. My sister and I thought it had burned down because the fire was right above it. When my mom got back to my grandma's house, the fire had jumped over the valley and onto Mount Ida. My grandma's place is at the foot of Mount Ida, and when mom arrived the fire was only 2 kilometres away. We had to evacuate grandma's place right away and go to my uncle's place on the other side of the mountain. We got there and evacuated them, and then we drove to another town about a half-hour away where friends of ours let the 13 of us stay in their house. We were out of our house for a whole month. I felt very scared and shocked, but was happy to be with my family and that we were safe.

Charles B. Smith
J.L. Jackson Junior Secondary School
Salmon Arm, British Columbia

ONTARIO MINISTRY OF NATURAL RESOURCES

A river snakes towards a fire at Red Lake, Ontario, 1985.

I go to bed about 1:30 a.m., exhausted but lucky. My home is on the northeast side of the town. I feel sick for those less fortunate than I. During the night, I awaken many times feeling frightened and worried about what the morning will bring. The winds finally calm down after midnight

The next day, Mr. McLeod's fears were justified.

I can see the flashing lights from the fire engines in the distance as the firefighters try to save houses. There is a continuous line of helicopter traffic from lake to fire as the fire nears the houses. After a few hours, I can see the fighters and helicopters slowly beat back the flames and push the fire away from the houses in this small corner of the wildfire.

The town sounds like a war zone, as the helicopters and water bombers work around the community throughout the day. There are flatbeds with heavy equipment parked in strategic locations in the town. The ground crews are amazing: I don't think I could do such back-breaking labour. Signs appear thanking the fighters for their efforts. The air and ground crews keep working hard and word arrives that 100 soldiers will arrive soon to fight the fire.

NATIONAL ARCHIVES OF CANADA/PA18399

Forest fire at Grand Rapids, Alberta, 1921.

A few days later, half the population of Salmon Arm — about 8,000 people — were put on a 10-minute evacuation alert, and evacuation centres were set up in the towns of Vernon, Sicamous, and Kamloops. It would be the largest evacuation in the history of British Columbia.

As the fire hovered near the southwest part of Salmon Arm, hundreds fled their homes. Downtown became a ghost town, and the RCMP were called in to protect against looting. In Salmon Valley, homes and outbuildings were burned to the ground while, inexplicably, neighbouring homes were untouched, illustrating the randomness of such fires.

Meanwhile, firefighters continued their battle with the fire and with the thick smoke that filled their lungs and stung their eyes. The town's community centre was kept open until 11 p.m. so weary firefighters could cool off in the pool and relax.

NATIONAL ARCHIVES OF CANADA/PA115262/CLAYSPERLING

Forest fire near Peshu Lake, Algoma District, Ontario, June 1948.

Twenty-one days after it began, the fire was declared under control, and the equipment and personnel began packing up, ready to be airlifted to another raging forest fire in another part of the country.

D'Arcy McLeod witnessed the farewell: "The Martin Mars water bombers circle the Salmon Arm bay and drop a load in the lake as they leave town," he wrote. "Impressive final fly-by as they leave to fight other fires. Hundreds of people were outside and saw this salute by the pilots — thank you. There are still 200 firefighters and 100 military up in the hills working on this monster. It won't be out until the snow flies."

ONTARIO MINISTRY OF NATURAL RESOURCES

Although this fire burned right to the edge of town, no structures were lost. Unfortunately, seven cottages in a subdivision north of the town were destroyed.

FORGOTTEN VICTIMS

In times of natural and manmade disasters, animals are often the forgotten victims. The Humane Society of Canada supplies animal feed, veterinary supplies, and funding to animals in disaster situations. We believe in assisting local communities with planning and, when disaster strikes, providing emergency assistance.

— Humane Society of Canada

CHAPTER 6

The Drought of 2001

June to September, 2001

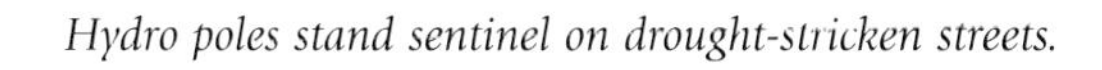

AGRICULTURE AND AGRI-FOOD CANADA — PFRA

Hydro poles stand sentinel on drought-stricken streets.

FOR THE RECORD

- This drought is considered worse than the droughts of 1961 and 1988
- $1.1 billion to $1.4 billion is expected to be paid out in crop insurance
- almost every province and territory in Canada was affected

Money can't buy everything. Friendship and learning to love and help others are what bring true happiness. When I look back on my life, I realize that I owe my beliefs, my relationships, and my life to the Dirty Thirties.

Joanne Abrams

St. George Elementary School

Saskatoon, Saskatchewan

NO SINGLE ELEMENT HAS A GREATER IMPACT ON THE WORLD THAN WATER. AS WE SAW in the chapter on floods, water is dangerous in its abundance. It can be equally lethal in its scarcity.

As it destroys crops and livestock, a drought's repercussions are many, from quality of life factors (food shortages, poverty, illness) to ecological factors (increased chance of forest fires, wind and soil erosion, fish, fowl, and wildlife habitat disturbances, poor air quality) to economic factors (higher food prices, income losses in other sectors directly and indirectly linked to agriculture, high unemployment, low gross national product).

Although droughts are far more deadly in other parts of the world, they are, nonetheless, a major hazard in Canada, both to our food and water supply and to our economic well-being. The drought of 1988, which was focused on the Prairies, caused a staggering $1.8 billion in damage.

AGRICULTURE AND AGRI-FOOD CANADA — PFRA

Parched landscapes and dry creek beds at the height of the drought.

Anatomy of a Disaster: The Drought of 2001

The summer of 2001 was an exceptionally dry one for most of Canada. Those of us in the city endured the heat by turning up our air conditioners and watching our lawns turn brown. But farmers across Canada weren't watching their lawns die — it was their livelihoods that were withering away.

After two dry years of low crop yields, Canadian farmers were hoping for a good season to make up for some of their losses. Instead, production of wheat, barley, canola, and soy was down an average of 25 percent from 2000, which had already shown the lowest yields since the drought of 1988. Many farmers were forced to sell their livestock, as poor pasture conditions and a lack of food and water meant that they would be unable to feed the animals over the winter.

The difficult growing season of 2001 was not simply due to a lack of rain; much of the problem was the poor distribution of rain. Parts of British Columbia and Manitoba received considerably more rain than usual, causing crops to rot in the fields. Southern Manitoba received between 350 and 500 mm of rain, more than three times its average rainfall. Alberta, Saskatchewan, Southern Ontario, Quebec, and much of the Maritimes, meanwhile, suffered from precipitation levels that, in the early summer, were about one-quarter of the average rainfall. Soil was dried almost to dust by temperatures hovering between 30 and 35°C. One of the worst-hit regions, the area around London, Ontario, received only 14.2 mm of rain for the entire month of July, one-fifth of its average of 76.7 mm. While precipitation levels increased marginally in August, it was too late for most farmers to save the season.

For those farmers already suffering from overextended finances, watching their potential income literally drying up was a disaster indeed. Over 4,000 people applied for government aid of some type, amounting to $13 million in claims. When combined with other assistance programs, total assistance to farmers amounted to $3.8 billion.

The drought did not hit everyone equally. Rising crop prices due to diminishing supply offset the losses for some farmers, and boosted the profit margins of those who were not too badly affected by the drought. With the help of government-assisted programs, the average Canadian farmer managed to make it through the season.

In the last 200 years, Canada has been struck by about 40 severe droughts — the most damaging ones being those in the 1890s, and in 1930, 1988, and 2001. Droughts are more prevalent in Western Canada, especially in an area called the Palliser Triangle, which comprises the southern parts of Alberta, Saskatchewan, and Manitoba. The Triangle was named after John Palliser, who explored the area in 1857 and deemed it unfit to farm. But the political agenda of the day — the Canadian Dream — superseded practical concerns: Immigrants were met at the boat and told to keep moving West. After successive crop failures, many of these settlers eventually began a migration of their own to more arable land or to cities.

When it comes to natural disasters in Canada,
There is nothing more I hate,
For example, the Red River Flood of '97
And the Drought of '88.

The damage they caused was lethal,
And very expensive to repair,
So before another one hits,
Be sure you've taken care
In getting protection against future losses
Due to natural disasters and calamaties.

Dermain Finlayson
Morning Star Middle School
Mississauga, Ontario

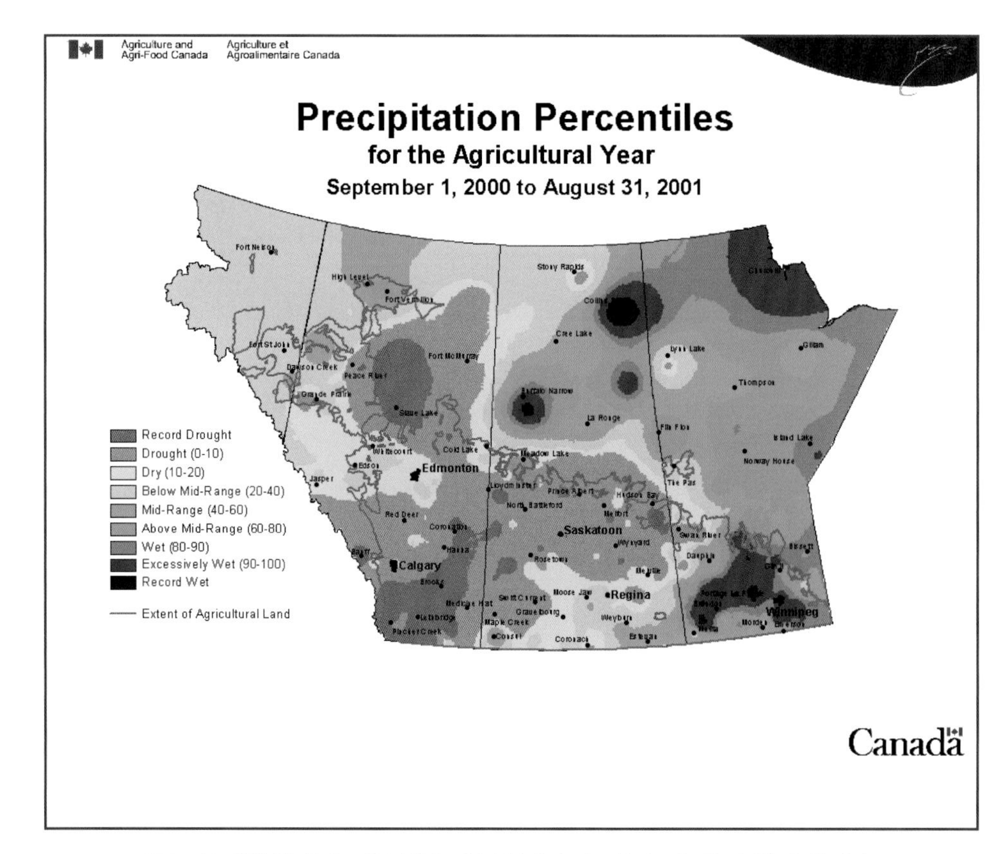

Prepared by PFRA (Prairie Farm Rehabilitation Administration) using data from the Timely Climate Monitoring Network and the many federal and provincial agencies and volunteers that support it.

Droughts are caused when shifts in the jet stream block storm systems and prevent them from reaching an area. These blockages can last for weeks, months, and even years. Moisture is sucked out of the soil, the air and the river beds, exacerbating the unbearable air temperatures. When the rains do come, it takes days and weeks of steady rain to begin to restore the land.

Without a doubt, farmers are my personal heroes. They are tenacious in their resolve to win, even when Mother Nature deals them a pathetic hand. They routinely go to Ottawa for assistance from the government's farm assistance programs, and are routinely jeered at and scorned by the public. No one seems to appreciate the monumental risks inherent in farming. It takes a lot of courage and a lot of risk to be a farmer. But the fact remains that someone has to plant and harvest, or we don't eat.

My heroes are not what most people's would be,
Because my heroes are just normal people, like you and me.
They don't have magical powers or fly through the night,
Nor do they save others in danger, at first sight.
I admire the suffering children of The Great Depression's Dust Bowl
Who struggled all their lives but continued to reach their goals.
It is these children who passed the message on
That we are fortunate people and can help those in harm.
If it weren't for them, I would never have come to know
That I am very fortunate and live in a safe place, where I have grown.
These kids had the courage and the outstanding faith
To strive through hard days with their non-quitting strength.
This bit of prairie history has taught me to observe
The world, and to question what is and what we all deserve.

Kathie Allen
Rideau Park School
Calgary, Alberta

AGRICULTURE AND AGRI-FOOD CANADA — PFRA

The Chin Reservoir, near Taber, Alberta, at 49% capacity. Note the distance from the water's edge to the boat dock.

In the summer of 2001, when the rains didn't materialize, agriculture began to spiral downwards. Devastating losses to crops and livestock were posted, and the extent of the disaster brought inevitable comparisons to the Dust Bowl of 1930s, considered the most serious emergency Canada has experienced.

But this particular drought was different: Almost every province and territory in Canada was affected by the parched conditions. Moncton, New Brunswick, for instance, which normally receives 102 millimetres of precipitation in July, recorded only 17.3 millimetres.

Farmers bonded from one end of the country to the other as they struggled with their crops under searing heat and relentlessly sunny skies. In British Columbia, forage crops were affected; in Alberta, ranchers ran out of feed for their cattle; in Saskatchewan, some farmers harvested as little as 20 percent of their normal yield; in Ontario, corn growth was stunted and soybean yields were low; in Quebec, pumpkins, apples, and soybeans withered in the heat; in New Brunswick, apples and blueberry yields were jeopardized; in Nova Scotia, bean yields were below average; in Prince Edward Island, broccoli and cauliflower crops were down, and the impact on the potato crop was deemed more destructive to that industry than the previous year's U.S. ban over potato wart; in Newfoundland, dry soil conditions resulted in poor strawberry yields and delayed the harvest by at least three weeks.

A farm in Lethbridge District with dwindling hay bale supplies. One bale will feed 100 head of cattle for only a day and a half. Many ranches had to truck in feed from the east.

AGRICULTURE AND AGRI-FOOD CANADA — PFRA

AGRICULTURE AND AGRI-FOOD CANADA — PFRA

St. Mary's Reservoir in southern Alberta at 29% capacity.

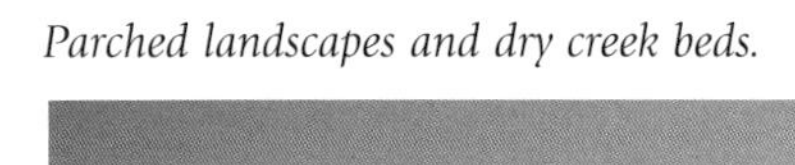

Parched landscapes and dry creek beds.

AGRICULTURE AND AGRI-FOOD CANADA — PFRA

In a move eerily reminiscent of events of the 1930s, Prairie farmers shipped entire herds hundreds of kilometres east to places not affected by the drought. In other areas, livestock was sold because of poor pasture conditions and inadequate water and feed.

And the dry weather wasn't just killing crops, it was killing valuable insects and spreading disease.

In central Canada, water levels in the Great Lakes fell: Lake Huron dipped 10 centimetres below the previous year's levels; Lake Superior was down 15 centimetres.

Psychologically, the drought exhausted those who depend on the soil for a living. Numerous farms fell into bankruptcy, and people spoke of effects on children whose parents were increasingly stressed and depressed.

Drought doesn't carry the cachet of other disasters. Drought is an inert disaster. There are no sounds, no crashing waves or screaming winds. The sight of dead and rotting cattle makes for powerful images on the nightly news, but it never propels us into action. A shrivelled berry in a farmer's hand has little effect on us, yet it is a harbinger of a bigger problem.

Soil drifting in the Lethbridge, Alberta, area.

AGRICULTURE AND AGRI-FOOD CANADA — PFRA

AGRICULTURE AND AGRI-FOOD CANADA — PFRA

The drought left pasturelands with little grass for cattle to feed on.

Oddly enough, we turn away from the problem rather than respond to it. There is little compassion shown to farmers, and that's very sad. As a country, we should rejoice at their bumper crops and quickly come to their aid when disaster strikes. Canada is capable of raising millions of dollars for drought-affected areas in other countries, but help needs to start at home. We must nurture and care for our own through a strategy that recognizes that the bread belt of Canada is, at times, subjected to extreme weather.

In a drought, there is little you can do but wait it out. While some farmers ploughed their fields under to prevent weeds from growing and to conserve whatever moisture was left in the soil, others simply began the tiresome and demoralizing task of applying for drought aid from Ottawa.

NATIONAL ARCHIVES OF CANADA/PA186321

Unloading carloads of hay for relief of farmers in drought-stricken areas near Sonnerfeld, Saskatchewan, in the 1930s.

AGRICULTURE AND AGRI-FOOD CANADA — PFRA

AGRICULTURE AND AGRI-FOOD CANADA — PFRA

Southern Alberta has been hit hard by several consecutive years of drought, with record dry conditions continuing through 2001 and into 2002. Area producers have struggled in the face of the region's worst dry spell in more than 63 years.

Conditions deteriorated during the critical growing months of summer, with just a small fraction of normal precipitation recorded in June, July, and August of 2001. By summer's end, the region had received only one-third of average precipitation for the first eight months of the year. Remarkably, there had not been a rainfall of more than 1 cm recorded at the Lethbridge airport for a period of more than two months. This followed on the heels of three very dry years with little in the way of runoff or mountain snowpack.

Many smaller creeks, streams, and water holes dried-up. The Waterton, St. Mary, and Milk Ridge reservoirs were all operating at less than one-third of capacity, while the Chin, Stafford, Forty Mile, Suder, Murray, Horsefly, and Grassy reservoirs were well under half of their capacity. In addition, area rivers were noticeably lower, and most dugouts — which provide a critical source of water to farming operations — were low to empty.

Dryland farmers and ranchers have been hardest hit. Cattle had to be sold due to little or no pasture growth. Some farmers allowed cattle into their crops — with yields so low it was economically preferable to use the crops as livestock feed. With pastures tinder dry throughout the area, a number of prairie fires developed. One such fire near Milk River encompassed an area of 30 kilometres by 10 kilometres.

The drought sparked a significant increase in demand for services from the Agriculture and Agri-Food Canada office serving the Lethbridge district. Requests for assistance ranged from piping water to empty dugouts and drilling wells where surface water had dried up to inquiries about where to get feed for cattle or how to get hooked up quickly to a local water co-op. In addition, a number of clients with dugouts that were not yet empty required assistance in dealing with deteriorating water quality (as dugout water evaporated, water mineral content, such as sulphates, increased).

With crop yields under these conditions projected to be 20–50% of average in most areas, many dryland producers and ranchers faced financial trouble. The situation will be compounded in the future if there is not significant rainfall and an abundant winter mountain snowpack.

The subsequent economic ripple effect is expected to be felt throughout the Lethbridge district, which is home to more than 10,000 farms (1996 est.) covering more than 6.5 million acres (2.6 million hectares), a large food processing industry, half of Alberta's irrigated lands, over half of Alberta's beef finishing industry, a large agri-business sector, one-third of Alberta's farm gate sales, one-fifth of Alberta's milk producers, and the highest density of intensive livestock operations in Canada. *— Agriculture and Agri-Food Canada — PFRA*

COURTESY BETTER FARMING MAGAZINE

Drought leaves soil hard and cracked. This corn crop won't make it to market.

CHAPTER 7

The Toronto Snowstorm

January 2, 1999

COURTESY THE WRIGHTS

Several days after the worst of the snow hit, many city streets were still difficult to drive on.

FOR THE RECORD

- 118.4 cm of snow fell, the largest accumulation of snow in Toronto in any month since records have been kept (city averages 130 cm per year)
- 2,300 people (800 city staff, 1,400 contract employees, 100 local reserves) helped clear snow
- 438 military personnel and 128 vehicles from CFB Petawawa assisted in the clean-up for two weeks
- $70 million was spent on clearing the snow

It began as a nice day with perfect weather. I was with three of my friends. We were playing hide and seek at the school. Later, we had a huge party with pizza, cake, hot dogs, and juice. Afterwards, we were ready to play outside, but when we opened the door all we saw was snow. It was a blizzard, a super blizzard. After a day, the blizzard finally ended.

Benjamin Kissock
Nakasuk Elementary School
Iqaluit, Nunavut

THE SNOWSTORM OF '99 WAS ACTUALLY TWO STORMS THAT HIT TORONTO IN QUICK succession. The first one hit on January 2, dumping 39 centimetres; two weeks later another 26 centimetres fell. It was a storm of such speed and density that the army was called in to help clear it away; a state of emergency was imposed, and Toronto Mayor Mel Lastman appeared on national television to say he was "terrified."

It was enough to prompt CBC's Rex Murphy to deliver one of his rants on *The National*: "It snowed in Ontario recently — and some of it fell on Toronto, a fair bit. And judging from the reaction, this is not only unusual, astonishing, and a great blathering horror, it's downright unnatural. Even as I speak, the trauma teams are assembling, snow counsellors are on 24-hour call, and the St. Bernards are being given Evian barrels and sensitivity training."

On December 17, 1995, my family and I were going to Nunavut's public library. It was snowing hard that afternoon. As I stepped outside, I felt the bitter wind chill my bones. The lights had gone out a half an hour before. We decided to go for a walk. I walked behind my mother so she could block out the white scenery. We got halfway when, as far as I know, my mother left the snow-covered road. I tried to ask what she was doing over the ear-piercing wind, when I heard a far-off sound. It sounded like a skidoo. It came with sounds of joy. It was my mother. I ran while my eyes searched ahead of me. There, before my eyes, were three skidoos! My family was on them. I jumped on. They brought us to someone's house and covered us in blankets.

Anika Aylward
Nakasuk Elementary School
Iqaluit, Nunavut

Anatomy of a Disaster: The Toronto Snowstorm of 1999

Shortly after Kangiqsualujjuaq was buried beneath an avalanche, Toronto panicked as two heavy snowstorms dropped a total of 65 cm of snow on the city within two weeks. Transportation ground to a halt, leaving many unable to attend work and thousands of people stranded at the airport on one of the busiest days of the year. The city's size proved a huge disadvantage as it set out to clear hundreds of kilometres of roads, using empty fields as dumps for the mountains of snow. Some of these man-made miniature glaciers were over 10 metres high and did not melt until late summer.

In the end, however, the city made it out of the storm. Much of Canada was amused at Toronto's concern, but on the heels of the ice storm that had frozen two provinces in their tracks the year before, this panic is understandable. After all, it is often difficult to tell the difference between a patch of bad weather and an impending disaster until the disaster has already struck.

What pushes bad weather into the realm of disaster? According to one scientist, disasters are mostly extreme weather out of context, whether by being in an unexpected place or in an unexpected quantity. A snowstorm that might be commonplace in Edmonton is disastrous in Toronto because the locals aren't prepared for that sort of weather. Similarly, the dams of the Saguenay could have held back much of the rain if they had been 5 metres taller, but no one expected such heavy rains.

Preparation is not the only factor, though it is a significant one. Ever-increasing population density means that when a disaster strikes, there are more people to be harmed, and more property to be destroyed. This is why many storms are breaking new records for destructiveness. Climate change means that we are seeing more and more storms striking in unexpected places, and these storms are often more intense. "We're going to see meteorological extremes more and more frequently," warned geologist Denis Roy after the Saguenay flood.

As with many survivors of disaster (or near disaster), Toronto has taken measures to ensure that it is not unprepared again, investing in heavy-duty snow-melting machines and removal equipment. Its preparation has allowed it to help its neighbours, too. Late in 2001, Toronto loaned its equipment to Buffalo, New York, when a snowstorm dumped 2 metres of snow on that city.

Although many do not consider the Toronto Snowstorm a natural disaster, 11 people died as a result of the storm, some felled by heart attacks as they tried to shovel their way out of their homes, others when the snow left them unable to receive proper medical care. That's more than the death toll of either the Red River or Saguenay floods, which proves that even a near disaster can take its toll.

TORONTO STAR/TONY BOCK

Clearing the tracks. Work crews clear snow off the tracks approaching Union Station.

But in defence of my city, I think it is important to take a broader look. Yes, when you are able-bodied and healthy such storms are fun — if nothing else, it gives everyone an excuse to stay home from work. But when you are disabled, frail, sick, or elderly, such storms are seen through a darker lens. They can be terrifying, and can exacerbate a person's sense of isolation.

When the first wave of the storm hit, the city was ill-prepared to deal with the deluge. Crews could not remove the snow fast enough, and traffic grounded to a halt. On some streets, snow piles were almost twice as high as people; many of those piles concealed cars, some of which remained buried for weeks. Transit systems were grounded when rail switches froze and cars were left abandoned on streetcar tracks.

But more troubling than the inability to get from one part of the city to another was the prospect of emergency situations: How could ambulances get critically ill people to the hospital when the city's streets were impassable?

TWN

I live in the city, but when I was out at my farm one night a sort of semi-blizzard hit the area and since most people on the road couldn't see three feet out of the windows of their cars, they had to pull over. Now, a car only has so much fuel, and heating a car depends on fuel. The storm went on for a while. My dad realized there may be a few people stuck on the roads, so we went out in our truck and brought some of these people to our farm. I think that helping people gives you a great feeling. If you ever get the chance, help someone.

Colin Tulloch
École W.S. Hawrylak School
Regina, Saskatchewan

One time, there was a big blizzard in our town. There was no school that day. The buses and taxis were off the road. Then there was an emergency! A lady named Amanda was ready to have her baby. She couldn't get to the hospital and the ambulance couldn't get to her house. So the doctor came to Amanda's house by skidoo. Akeeshoo's uncle Eegeesiak, who was a volunteer firefighter, brought Dr. Brown to Amanda's house. Amanda's husband and mom helped Dr. Brown deliver the baby. They wrapped the new baby in warm towels from the clothes dryer. They named the baby Katlin.

Aggiuq Ashoona, Levi Kho, Mary Inookee,
Josephie Naglingniq, Edward Qaqqasiq,
Tai Qiatsuq
Nakasuk Elementary School
Iqaluit, Nunavut

My most amazing experience was when our door was blocked by snow for three days. We were stuck inside the house. My uncle finally shovelled for us.

Aveena Angrove
Nakasuk Elementary School,
Iqaluit, Nunavut

When I was eight, there was a blizzard. I had to walk home in the blizzard. I kept falling down because it was slippery. My face was cold and my eyebrows were frozen.

Clifford Bourgaize
Nakasuk Elementary School
Iqaluit, Nunavut

I love blizzards because the snow gets really high and we can build snow forts. I got stuck in my snow fort, so my sister had to break it in half. I got a lot of snow down my neck.

Devin Peeteetuce
Nakasuk Elementary School
Iqaluit, Nunavut

The dilemma was solved when soldiers from the Canadian Forces base in Petawawa, near Ottawa, arrived with several Bisons — huge armoured vehicles designed to traverse all sorts of conditions on a battlefield.

Norm Ferrier, a senior emergency planner with Toronto's Emergency Medical Service, says that lives were saved due to the presence of the soldiers and their co-operative work with paramedics.

"Two paramedics were put on each Bison, along with the soldiers, and the vehicles were sent out into the streets to respond to emergency calls that regular ambulances could not reach. The vehicles were equipped with two-way radios and were assigned to 911 calls by the Emergency

COURTESY TWN

On Friday, January 28, 1977, a natural disaster struck parts of southern Ontario. Temperature and wind combined to create a wind chill of 60 degrees below zero. The storm did not stop until February. Wind gusts of more than 50 miles per hour appeared each day with peaks ranging between 69 and 73 miles per hour. By the night of January 28, thousands of people were stranded. Snowmobilers volunteered their time to help stranded children and other needy citizens. They worked with radio stations to deliver emergency items. The entire Regional Municipality of Niagara was placed in a state of emergency on January 29; it stayed in effect until February 2. If there are lessons to be learned from the survival of others, learn them. It could happen again. It could happen to you.

Chris Tobey and Michael McRae

Prince Philip Public School • Niagara Falls, Ontario

After school, I went to my grandmother Kathleen's house. I walked, and it was really cold. There was a blizzard. I was so cold that my hands and feet froze. I kept on walking, hoping someone would pick me up. I started to run. Sometimes, I saw snowmobiles drive by. I was getting closer to my grandmother's house. There was a lot of snow, and I was sinking as I ran. I got closer and closer, and then I finally made it. I went inside my grandmother's house and I took off my hat, gloves, shoes, and coat. There was snow all over my pants. I sat near a heater because my feet were still cold. After I melted, I had a cup of tea. I had to stay at my grandmother's house because there was no way to get home.

Louie Rich

Peenamin McKenzie School

Sheshatshiu, Labrador

With two Home Depot employees who assisted seniors and the physically challenged during the '99 Toronto snowstorm.

How wonderful the town looked in May 1985 covered in a fresh blanket of fluffy white snow with more falling from the sky. No one knew how bad the snow could be. It snowed all day, and in the evening a horrible storm began. Thinking the storm would pass, everyone went to sleep, all except for the people who drove the snowplows. They were struggling to keep the roads clear. Their efforts didn't help much. In the morning, the people woke up to see that their homes were buried in snow. When they turned on their radios to hear how bad the storm was they heard that half the town was, buried in snow. Someone had the idea of putting the snow on the lake. The town was saved.

Kallie Shires • Queen of Peace School
Leamington, Ontario

Medical Services (EMS) dispatch centre. It was quickly realized that the Bisons were too large to fit into the city's EMS stations, and so arrangements were made with the fire department. Between calls, the Bison would go to fire stations so that crews could rest. The vehicles would also be made available to the fire department, to carry firefighters to any call that a fire engine could not reach. This teamwork approach would last throughout the storm and in the days that followed."

Bison "ambulances" responded to calls from heart attack victims in narrow, snow-filled streets downtown and rescued those stranded in off-road locations such as ravines and parks.

Once again, the Canadian Forces proved valuable in helping those on its home turf.

COURTESY NATIONAL DEFENCE IMAGE LIBRARY

Canadian Armed Forces Personnel Carrier — The "Bison."

In May, 1985, a hailstorm surprised everyone across Leamington. It was very sudden and extremely odd. It lasted for five minutes. The pellets of hail were large. The quantity was considerable and the damage to vehicles, greenhouses, crops and rooftops was extensive. A storm that lasts only five minutes can last a lifetime in our memories.

Lisa Rutgers
Queen of Peace School
Leamington, Ontario

During the Toronto snowstorm of 1998, I went to residents who live on my street. I asked if they wanted me to snowblow the snow on their driveways and side-walks for $1 per house. I made $50. I gave $30 of that money to the Hospital for Sick Children.

Dino Novielli
Ascension of Our Lord Secondary School
Mississauga, Ontario

We looked out the window and saw a blizzard. I went upstairs and got a game, and we started to play. All of a sudden, the power went out. It was a blackout. No, it was a whiteout. We lit some candles and waited until the lights came back on.

Colin Parker
Nakasuk Elementary School
Iqaluit, Nunavut

When I went outside it was cold, and there was a whiteout. I couldn't see a thing, and I was shivering. I went inside my house and called my friends and asked if they wanted to play outside. We made a big tunnel near my house.

Jimmy Ipeelie
Nakasuk Elementary School
Iqaluit, Nunavut

I saw a cool blizzard. After I had breakfast, I got dressed warmly, and then I went to play outside. I went to pick up Alex and Ooleepeeka. We had so much fun.

Kimberly Bouchard
Nakasuk Elementary School
Iqaluit, Nunavut

I love blizzards because I can stay at home. I wanted to go to school, but it was stormy and my mom had to stay in the house with my two little sisters and me. My dad went outside to chop wood. My sisters and I went outside. It was a nine-day blizzard. It was so cool because my sisters and I were able to go skidooing.

Dayna Curley-Tatty
Nakasuk Elementary School
Iqaluit, Nunavut

Normally, Construction Volunteers Canada doesn't get involved in snowstorms because they are not true disasters; we save our volunteers for those in dire need.

But CVC still got calls. I remember one woman from the well-heeled neighbourhood of Rosedale calling and demanding we assist her immediately in repairing her door. And City Hall has pages of complaints from angry residents upset about not being able to move around the city. Some people expect to get the same level of service regardless of the weather.

When I woke up there was a blizzard outside. I built a tunnel and played for a few hours.

Myles Gauthier
Nakasuk Elementary School
Iqaluit, Nunavut

The worst blizzard I ever saw was a two-day whiteout in Clyde River. The power was on; however, we could only get three channels on television. The next day the power went out. We lit some candles and my family and I played board games.

Jacques Hainnu
Nakasuk Elementary School
Iqaluit, Nunavut

Once, when I was five, we had a blizzard. I had to go to my aunt's house. I forgot my hat and I got frostbite. The next day I woke up, and my ear was hurting. I told my mom. Later, I had to go to the hospital to have minor surgery on my ear, but it is fine now.

Jennifer Anne Ipeelie
Nakasuk Elementary School
Iqaluit, Nunavut

It was –15° here in Iqaluit. Everybody was freezing like crazy and making fires in their fireplaces. Taxi service was out and you had to walk everywhere. Suddenly, the temperature dropped to –40°. I invited my friend, Gustin, over to play outside with me.

Taylor Roberts
Nakasuk Elementary School
Iqaluit, Nunavut

The worst blizzard we've ever been in was in Igloolik in 1998. I had to go home during the middle of school. I had to hold my brother's arm all the way home. The power went out. The next morning, I went downstairs and looked outside. It was still a blizzard. I was unhappy because I couldn't go to school.

Teresa Inooya
Nakasuk Elementary School
Iqaluit, Nunavut

But there were also heart-warming stories that showed how people could muster community spirit. Among my favourite is the action taken by Home Depot. I accompanied the employees when they went out to shovel snow for cancer patients, the physically challenged, and seniors.

TWN

A whiteout is a condition in Arctic regions in which a blending of snow and clouds produce a uniform milky whiteness characterized by the absence of shadow and the invisibility of all but very dark objects. I don't like whiteouts!

Kyle Arnold-Ashoona

Nakasuk Elementary School

Iqaluit, Nunavut

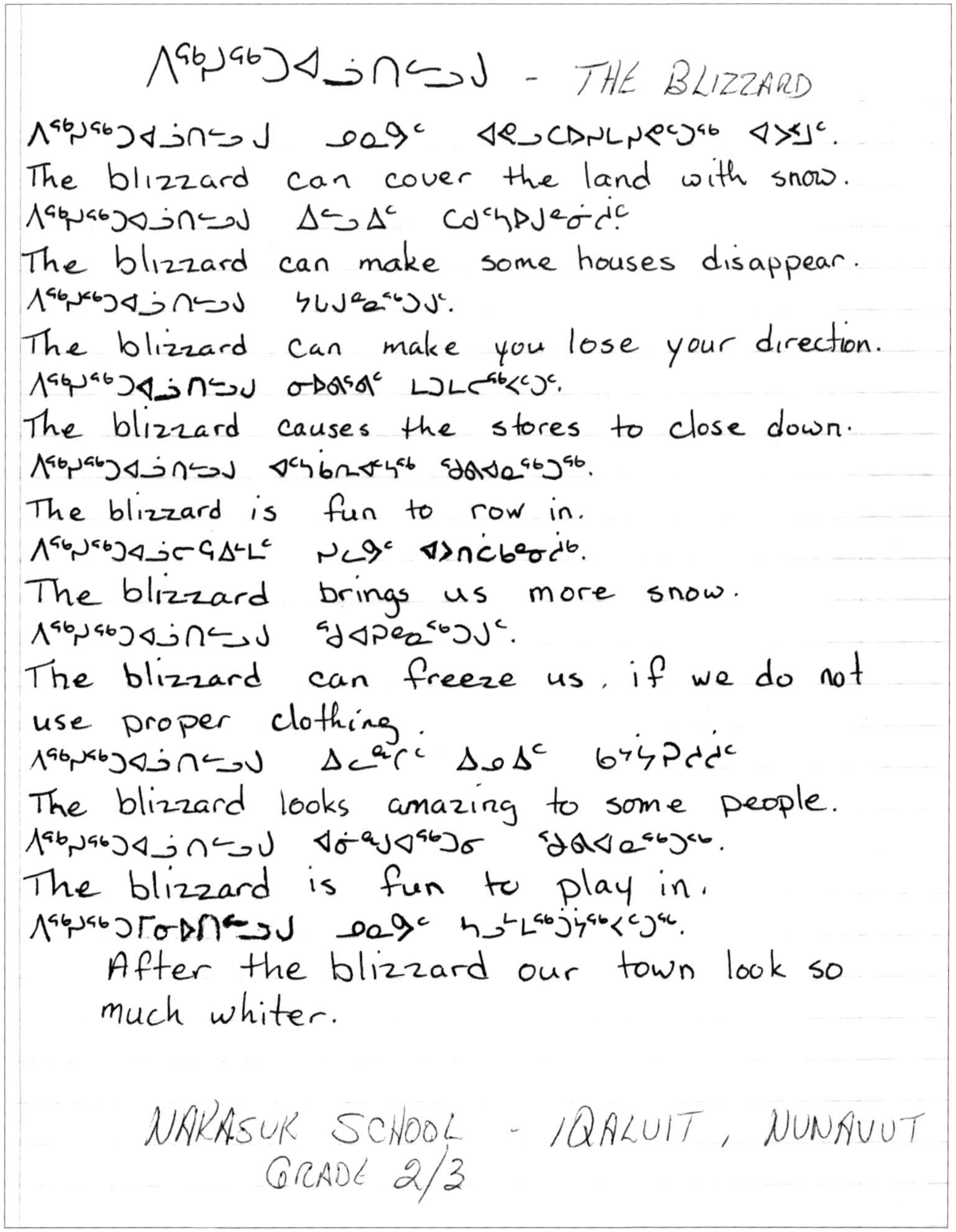

THE BLIZZARD

The blizzard can cover the land with snow.
The blizzard can make some houses disappear.
The blizzard can make you lose your direction.
The blizzard causes the stores to close down.
The blizzard is fun to row in.
The blizzard brings us more snow.
The blizzard can freeze us, if we do not use proper clothing.
The blizzard looks amazing to some people.
The blizzard is fun to play in.
After the blizzard our town look so much whiter.

NAKASUK SCHOOL - IQALUIT, NUNAVUT
GRADE 2/3

Dedicated to late Nakasuk School principal Hal Richards.

The wind was cold and strong. The snow was deep, and I made a tunnel. I got my sled and my friends came to play. We made a snowman. We had fun having snowball fights. When the blizzard got strong, we went into the tunnel.

Daniel Caza
Nakasuk Elementary School
Iqaluit, Nunavut

And even other cities and provinces helped out. Prince Edward Island sent 15 large snow blowers and two crews of operators to assist in the clean-up; help also came from London, Bracebridge, and Ottawa, Ontario, and Montreal, Quebec.

The snowstorm was not a major disaster, but it did cause panic and throw the city into chaos. Yet, in a pinch, even Toronto's critics helped out.

Blizzards have strong winds. We have to stay in the house, and when it's over we can go out to play. We make tunnels and have snowball fights. When I go to my room to sleep I can't sleep because of the howling winds. I then cover my ears and close my eyes, and I can fall asleep.

Amy Tikivik

Nakasuk Elementary School

Iqaluit, Nunavut

It all started in May, a long time ago.
It was nice outside when the wind began
to blow.
White balls of ice came crashing down,
Which was shocking to us all.
A hailstorm in May in our tiny town
Did not seem right at all.

Alicia Remark
Queen of Peace School
Leamington, Ontario

It struck on a cold winter night.
It brought the town of Leamington
quite a fright.
Stuck in one place, with nowhere to go,
The streets were slippery,
and piled with snow.
Children were cold,
and fires grew old.

Sarah Krahn
Queen of Peace School
Leamington, Ontario

On December 11, 1992, my dad and I were driving home from the store. The car was sliding all over the place. Suddenly, there was no place to go. The plough hadn't been down the street and we were stuck. What were we going to do? We looked around for house lights. Off in the distance we saw Christmas lights. We walked for what seemed like forever. We passed cars in the ditch and cars that had just pulled off the road. There was no one in the cars. We got to the house and knocked on the door. An elderly gentleman answered the door. We could hear people laughing and could smell food cooking. It sounded like a party. We told the man what had happened. He said to come in and warm up by the fire. He explained that everyone there had been stranded in some way by the storm. He said they had heard that the city had pulled their vehicles off the road because the weather was too dangerous for even them to be out on the roads. It could be tomorrow before they were ploughed. "Call your family and tell them you're fine and not to worry," he said. "We have lots of food and space for everyone. When the snow stops we'll help everyone get out." When we got home the next day, I had so much to tell my mom and sister. The big snow-storm of '92 was the best time I ever had.

Jessica Mooney and Lindsay Spencer
King Edward Public School • Peterborough, Ontario

COURTESY THE WRIGHTS

Faced with some of the worst snow conditions in a lifetime, most Torontonians remained in good humour.

In April 1997, my family and I went to visit my dad's friend in Winnipeg. While we were there it started snowing — in April, can you imagine that? This was followed by a blizzard. We were stuck at their house for three days. It got so bad that people were stranded in their cars and had to be rushed to the hospital suffering from hypothermia. Store owners and workers were also stuck at their workplaces for a couple of days. In fact, the roof of one store caved in leaving people in despair. It was a scary sight, but it was comforting to know that I was with my family and friends.

Harpreet Brar

Morning Star Middle School • Mississauga, Ontario

"The Ice Captive" — The Hamilton Snowstorm of 1898

Icy, raw winds blast from every angle,
Burning the skin of every man, woman, and child.
I am as though one dead,
I tread the cold and icy breeze and see the faces of many.
As though I was dreaming, I am in a house with other people.
They see me not.
There is a mother holding her small child, who won't stop
crying.
A father is leaning on a wall,
A little girl with hair of gold sleeps by a small fire.
She barely breathes.
An icy blow rocks the house and I am sent pitching, aimlessly.
I see that the town has lost its power,
Power lines are strewn and broken,
And mountainous trees, too brittle to withstand the wind,
Are snapped as though they were twigs in a child's hands.
I see another place now,
I am in it.
Once again I remain unseen.
There are people crying.
As I draw near, I see a mother covering a small, shivering boy.
He appears to be very cold and very sick.
I notice the mournful look on her face.
She fears for him because he is sick.
I leave the mournful place with another pitching breeze.
Snow and ice are blasting,
Raw winds are howling,
Men are moaning in frozen anguish,
Women and children weep for their loved ones who are sick,
Perhaps beyond cure.
My whole world pitches and twirls,
I see only brief images of people mourning,
Children crying.
I am as though one dead,
I walk on the raw wind.
I see and feel not, I am dreaming a strange dream.
It is like being in a familiar place with strangers.
I am realizing now that the town,
The whole city, is in the icy clutches of an ice storm,
As though it is being held hostage.
It is a prisoner,
A captive,
This town is the Ice Captive.

Eva Coruzzi
St. Jerome Catholic School
Hamilton, Ontario

They went home for lunch that day in
May,
Staring outside in great dismay.
The West was black. The East was bright
The South brought wind and quite a
fright.
They watched helplessly as the conditions combined,
The hail roared down, hope left behind.
It destroyed land, vehicles, and greenhouse glass,
Everyone was hoping that the storm
would soon pass.
It lasted only five minutes but seemed
like a day,
The destructive hail drove all creatures
away.
It is now 17 years later, and you all did
survive,
But no one will ever forget the hailstorm
of 1985.

Marlene Mastronardi
Queen of Peace School
Leamington, Ontario

Hail comes without warning
Breaking through the town,
Smashing anything as it falls to the
ground.
The hail so white and cold to touch
Hard and wet and far too much.

Breanna Kersey
Queen of Peace School
Leamington, Ontario

NATIONAL ARCHIVES OF CANADA/C35838/EDWIN A. GAVILLER

Hamilton snowstorm, December 1898.

TORONTO STAR/RICK MADONICK

Where's that hydrant? Pixie, a German boxer sporting a special collar to keep her from chewing at her post-operative stitches, nosed around a snow pile on Kingston Road following the storm.

CHAPTER 8

The Raging Seas

Tidal Waves, Surges, Gales, and Ice Floes

EASTERN GRAPHIC, SOURIS, PEI

Water levels rose to more than 4 feet over the top of the wharf during the tidal surge that struck the Souris wharf in Prince Edward Island in 2000.

FOR THE RECORD

- the Saxby Gale of October 4–5, 1869, was fed by hurricane-force winds; the surge that followed, a forceful dome of wind-driven waters, reached 2 metres above previous records, drowning dozens of people and animals
- 28 people were killed when a tidal wave hit the Burin Peninsula of Newfoundland in 1929; more than 100 fishing boats and 26 schooners were wrecked, and approximately 500 buildings were destroyed
- 58 homes and businesses were destroyed by the tsunami that hit Alberni and Port Alberni, British Columbia, on March 27–28, 1964
- a tidal surge hit Prince Edward Island on January 21, 2000
- according to Environment Canada, between 10,000 and 40,000 icebergs prowl Canadian waters every year

The 1929 Tidal Wave

In 1929, on the Burin Peninsula of Newfoundland, the townspeople experienced a force of nature quite unusual to the area.

My great grandmother, who was living in the small fishing community of Port Au Bras, was witness to the terrible onslaught.

It was a cool, autumn evening on November 18. Everyone was diligently doing their evening chores with no idea of the disaster that lay in store for this small peninsula.

About 5 p.m. the area was hit by an earthquake. Everything rattled and shook. Most people at this time had no knowledge of things such as earthquakes and were left not knowing what had happened. It was only the beginning.

Debris from the 1929 tidal wave that hit the Burin Peninsula, November 1929.

NATIONAL ARCHIVES OF CANADA/C26492

Radio had not yet reached this area, so there was no way for the people to be warned of the upcoming event that would change most of their lives. At about 8 p.m. the water drained completely out of the harbour. There had been a high tide for a while, but when this happened people definitely took notice. Shortly after the water had receded, the tidal wave came with tremendous force.

The coastline was ravaged, and many people were left without even a second to react. Many fled to high land. This saved many lives. Two more waves followed the first, and each was of comparable intensity. When the waves had ceased, people came out of hiding and surveyed the damage. While the water was calm, everything else was destroyed. Houses and wharves had been completely carried away, and the harbour was filled with debris. Winter provisions had been swept away, and everyone was in awe of the awesome force that had assaulted their peninsula. The fishing grounds had been swept clean of any marine life, and it would take more than 10 years for the fishing to return to normal.

It is often said of Newfoundlanders that they are kind, generous, and helpful people. This was proved over and over through donations and volunteer labour.

— Melissa Dawe,
St. Michael's School, Goose Bay, Labrador

Anatomy of a Disaster: The Raging Seas

Canadians are often awe-struck by the beauty of the seas, but we must also be aware of their capacity for destruction. The Maritimes are constantly battered by severe weather, from violent winds and raging tides to May snowstorms. Those who endure this harsh climate are heroes by example and models of determination for many of us. However, occasionally the seas can bring storms so terrible that even Maritimers are unprepared.

Because much of Canada's coastline is arctic, icebergs and ice floes are a perpetual risk. Anyone who has heard of the *Titanic* knows of the danger of icebergs. Ice floes — slowly shifting glaciers — can be a serious hazard to arctic travellers, especially to ship navigators, who are relying on maps of a landscape that is slowly changing.

Strong nautical windstorms are known as gales. These storms can bring hard rains and tidal surges, which pose a dangerous flood risk to coastal regions. The Saxby Gale was named after Stephen Martin Saxby, who had been watching weather patterns and predicted that a severe storm would combine with a high tide to produce disastrous results sometime between October 5 and 9, 1869. On October 4, weather watchers noticed the barometer dropping rapidly, indicating a violent storm on the horizon. The gale caused a tidal surge — a sudden rise in ocean levels. This 2-metre surge coincided with an exceptionally high tide, a phenomenon of planetary alignment with the sun and moon that occurs only once every 18 years. The combined force led to severe flooding all along the coast. Those who had heeded Saxby's warnings were glad they had done so.

Tsunamis are commonly known as tidal waves, but the name is deceiving. These giant and destructive waves have nothing to do with tides; they are more like shock waves, the result of a dramatic impact. Most tsunamis, such as the one that hit Burin Peninsula in 1929, are due to earthquakes. Unfortunately, it is still almost impossible to predict the direction in which a tsunami will travel and the size to which it will build. Scientists are working on new techniques of prediction so that appropriate emergency measures can be taken when an earthquake shakes the ocean floor.

In sheer size and destructive power, hurricanes are the most mighty and terrible of all storms. Known as typhoons and cyclones in the Indian subcontinent, hurricanes form in the low latitudes of tropical oceans. When summer heats the ocean's surface, the warm, humid air forms clouds and thunderstorms, which continue to build as they encounter the low-pressure troughs that drift west along the equator. The earth's spin curves the winds around the central low pressure. As this spinning becomes consistent, a relatively calm eye develops in the middle, surrounded by spiral bands of rain. Once the winds reach about 120 km/hour, the storm is considered a hurricane.

The Saxby Gale

The Saxby Gale occurred on October 4 and 5, 1869. At 5 p.m. on October 4, the telegraph lines were down to the west of the Saint John newspaper office, and by 7 p.m. the winds continued to blow and the rains came pelting down. The wind was so strong that it blew light and loose materials everywhere and shook the old houses. Gates and other objects were tossed about as if they were paper.

A news story of the time reported that approximately 100 people were killed; numerous livestock were drowned, and acres of land flooded. The Saxby Gale became known as "the storm of the century."

Near Hillsborough, New Brunswick, the Gale brought a tragic end to the lives of four children. The flood waters rose so high that they surrounded the home of the O'Brian family, and it became impossible for them to escape, except by water. Mr. O'Brian was able to construct a makeshift raft from what lumber was drifting by. Soon Jacob O'Brian, his wife, and four children left on the raft in the hope that they would reach the opposite shore of the Petitcodiac River. In the middle of the river, the raft parted and the four children were drowned. Mr. O'Brian and his wife survived the ordeal, but their children were lost. Only three of the four children's bodies were ever recovered. As was typical in smaller communities in the region at the time, young and old alike pitched in to help those in need.

IVAN H. CROWELL/COURTESY UNIVERSITY OF NEW BRUNSWICK/TAPESTRY DESIGN MICHAEL McEWING

— Kayla Akerly, Siobhan Brown, and Kristen Parker, Hillsborough Elementary School, New Brunswick

CONSTRUCTION VOLUNTEERS CANADA HAS REACHED OUT DURING floods, the Ice Storm, and other natural disasters, but so far our relief efforts have been confined to inland disasters. Canada, however, has the longest coastline of any country in the world, and as such is prone to various naval disasters. Canada has a long history of tidal surges, tsunamis (tidal waves), gales, and hurricanes. The most famous Canadian hurricane, Hurricane Hazel, reached far inland, killing 81 people. Though storms such as Hazel do not hit us that often, smaller, but no less dangerous, storms and other sea disasters occur in this country every year.

What is most frightening about naval disasters is what could happen. The tsunami that hit Alberni and Port Alberni, British Columbia, in March 1964 cut a wide swath across the landscape, destroying dozens of businesses and homes. Still, no deaths were reported as a result of the disaster. The tidal wave that hit the Burin Peninsula of Newfoundland in 1929, on the other hand, killed many unsuspecting residents and demolished fishing boats and buildings. The wave was spawned by an earthquake that measured 7.2 on the Richter scale, the epicentre of which occurred hundreds of miles south of St. John's. Many were saved when they realized that the harbour had become nearly dry, and ran for higher ground — the burgeoning tidal wave had pulled the water from the harbour out to sea as it built itself up to a 30-metre wave before crashing on shore, eliminating wharves, residences, and boats. I hope never to have to rush to the scene of a town levelled by a tidal wave.

PHOTO COURTESY JOY CUMMINGS DICKINSON

Teacher, pewtersmith, master weaver, Ivan H. Crowell (b. 1904), a native of Nova Scotia was a teacher for several years. In 1940, he became director of handicrafts at McGill University, and in 1946, he moved to Fredericton and became director of handicrafts for New Brunswick. In 1969, Dr. Crowell studied pewtercraft and became the first pewtersmith in Canada. In 1973, he was named a member of the Order of Canada, and in 1977, he received the Queens Silver Jubilee Medal. Dr. Crowell has woven over 250 tapestries. One of those tapestries, on the Saxby Gale, appears on p. 156.

Caught on a Floe

Two Inuit elders, their eight-year-old grandson, a hunter, a science teacher, 11 high school students from Pond Inlet, Nunavut, and a parent of one of the students, started out on a biology-related field trip on June 1, 1997. They were planning to meet a similar group from Arctic Bay that included a marine biologist from Vancouver.

The Pond Inlet group travelled more than 100 kilometres the first day as they drove their snowmobiles, pulling heavy loads on their kamutiqs (long sleds) across the sea ice between Baffin Island and Bylot Island. Things were going well as they passed by seals sunning themselves, icebergs of incredible beauty, and the stunning vista of the mountains of Bylot Island. After driving all day and night (night, during the Arctic springtime, is brilliant sunlight) and making numerous stops for tea along the way, they finally set up camp at 6 a.m. Monday and went to sleep.

By mid-afternoon, they were on their way again towards Lancaster Sound, the mouth of the Northwest Passage. Minutes after skidooing onto Lancaster Sound, while feeling secure that all was well, they saw open water straight ahead. The lead skidoos immediately turned around, abruptly turning the kamutiqs in line. The ice that had been joined to the land had broken free and the group now found themselves on a large ice floe drifting further and further away.

They made radio contact with people in Pond Inlet and the Emergency Management Organization (EMO) went into action, setting up their headquarters at the hamlet office.

The Canadian Forces, RCMP, the families of the group, and the community were kept up to date. Elders were asked for their advice, and a team of people experienced at surviving in arctic conditions was assembled with the appropriate gear, including 12- to 15-foot-long boats, which were strapped on top of kamutiqs. The loads were heavy, but the men were confident that they could get to the place were the ice had broken free from the land. They would then have a chance to get to the group by boat if conditions permitted.

To make matters worse, a storm struck the area. The rescue team had to stop their journey until the strong winds had died down. The weather also prevented a helicopter from being sent to the stranded group.

The elders on the ice floe moved the group to multi-year ice, which is more secure than the first-year ice that they had been on. With the wind really picking up, they couldn't get all of the tents pitched. There wasn't enough room for everyone in the tents, so some students got into a large wooden box on top of a kamutiq and just threw a tent over it. The teacher was in a sleeping bag outside the box on the kamutiq with just the flapping tent for cover.

The next day, polar bear tracks were seen near the group's camp on the ice floe. It must have walked by during the storm while everyone was trying to sleep. It was less windy now, but the waves were breaking up the ice at the edges of the floe and were getting closer. The elders had everyone pack up their gear and move to a larger piece of older ice farther away from the edge. One student had brought a GPS, which allowed them to track, by satellite, the direction that they were drifting. They were now 30 to 40 km from land. The radio was still working, but the batteries were getting low. They had enough of most other supplies to last a few more days.

Although the weather was improving near the camp, there was freezing rain at the community where the helicopter was housed, which resulted in more delays. Rough water and the increasing distance from land prevented the local rescue team from heading out with boats. On Wednesday the weather had not improved. By this time some students were fearful and homesick, some parents were anxious, and everyone was concerned and praying. The drama out on the ice was being reported by the RCMP to the media. The impending disaster made international headlines.

A Hercules airplane from Trenton, Ontario, using the co-ordinates from the student's GPS, and with a little help from the smoke created by the deliberate burning of some caribou skins, was able to locate the group and drop supplies to them. A helicopter finally arrived from Iqaluit, and left Pond Inlet early Thursday morning, but returned shortly after as it had run into freezing rain.

On Thursday afternoon, the helicopter again made a rescue attempt. This time they were successful. Everyone on the ice was happy and filled with excitement and relief. They had drifted about 90 km from land.

All of the skidoos, kamutiqs, tents, sleeping bags, stoves, and other gear had to be left behind, as there was only enough room for the 16 people and a few of their personal belongings. Everything left behind was never seen again, at a loss of about $50,000. Things can be replaced. People cannot.

As the helicopter landed and the people got off, the hundreds of community members gathered at the airport began to clap, cheer, and cry. The group was warmly welcomed back home.

— David Parks, teacher, with Abbass Park
Nasivvik High School
Pond Inlet, Nunavut

On January 21, 2000, a combination of high tides and the storm surge increased the tidal water by 1 or 2 metres. That caused the dunes to collapse. At the Souris Harbour, a few of the fishermen's bait sheds were damaged by the water.

"We were very lucky," Souris fisherman Charlie Robichaud said. "The water was at least a metre higher than the high tides Souris normally has."

Katelyn Mahar
Eastern Kings Consolidated School
Souris, Prince Edward Island

The Navy Helps Make Bad Times Bearable

Good Bears of the World (Canada) is the name, giving teddy bears to children under stress or experiencing trauma is the aim. The Navy's scoring a bull's-eye.

In 2000, the Mississauga, Ontario, organization distributed 9,700 bears to 63 agencies — hospitals, shelters, fire and police departments, ambulances — across Canada.

Now, working with Maritime Forces Atlantic Public Affairs Officer Lieutenant (N) Pat Jessup, Good Bears has sent hundreds of bears to Canadian Forces Base Halifax, to be carried by CF personnel and distributed wherever they encounter children who could use the comfort of a teddy bear, in Canada and around the world.

"We never dreamed we'd be giving teddy bears at the federal level," said Andrew Cotterell, director of Good Bears of the World (Canada). "We were very excited to get a call from the Navy, and now there's a year-round program for the next 10 years in the making."

Mr. Cotterell and Deborah Fairlie, of Toronto, and Frank Glenn, of Oakville, are the directors of Good Bears of the World (Canada). The non-profit organization has six directors designate, ready to step in as directors when needed, and eight official advisors representing some of the larger groups distributing the organization's bears. Good Bears sets up displays at major shows in the Toronto area, fielding questions, accepting donated bears, and getting the particulars of groups needing bears.

"People will stop by, and a week or two later we'll get a call and find out they're Girl Guide or Boy Scout leaders or teachers, and they've gone out and collected bears for us," Mr. Cotterell said. "When the average Canadian hears what the Navy does for children in general, they're very proud. People who were there Friday night come back Sunday with bears, saying, 'Give these to the Navy.' It makes them and us proud to be Canadians."

— Ruthanne Urquhart,
Maple Leaf

LIEUTENANT (N) GARY HUSSEY, CFB HALIFAX

HMCS Charlottetown*'s Cpl Mike Brown, left, and PO2 Mark Bearss are obvious choices as bearsitters.*

Crewmembers of HMCS Charlottetown *welcome aboard a second crew of goodwill ambearsadors.*

LIEUTENANT (N) GARY HUSSEY, CFB HALIFAX

Terror at Sea

The beguiling calm of the waters of Frobisher Bay in Nunavut can suddenly change into a fury of angry waves that lash out at intruders cresting its space. Several years ago, during late fall, Simonie Alainga, an elder and a community leader, went walrus hunting with his relatives. It was traditional for Simonie to hunt for the community of Apex and Iqaluit. When they left Iqaluit, Frobisher Bay was calm. Conditions were ideal for a walrus hunt. Ten people looked forward to a successful hunt. At the end of the hunt, their boat was full of walrus.

On their return trip to Iqaluit, weather conditions suddenly worsened. The wind picked up, huge waves battered their boat. One of the men used his radio to ask his father, who lived on an outpost camp, to radio hunters and trappers for help. A search party set out. Unfortunately, they didn't know exactly where Simonie and his men were battling the waves.

Four days later a plane from search and rescue spotted two men clinging to a raft. Miraculously, they had survived the freezing waters. They were rescued. Eight others did not make it back to Iqaluit.

People were in shock. Friends and relatives from across Nunavut and the Northwest Territories offered help and support to the grieving families and the communities of Apex and Iqaluit. A memorial service was held for the eight who died. The Anglican cathedral was too small to hold the overflowing mourners. Messages of condolences and help to the survivors' dependants were received from countries as far as South Korea.

— Heather Michael-Graham (student) and H. Slaavid (school principal),
Nanook School
Apex, Nunavut

During the January tidal surge on P.E.I., my family and a friend were at the North Lake Harbour. There were a lot of icebergs in the harbour that came in with the high tide. Dad said the water was as high as he had ever seen it. The water was so high that some of the ice in the harbour actually floated onto the wharf. I am very concerned about tidal surges because if the waves or icebergs get really big, they could wipe out houses or buildings around the lake.

Andrew Rose
Eastern Kings Consolidated School
Souris, Prince Edward Island

Nautical disasters have plagued our country since Confederation. The *Empress of Ireland* went down in the St. Lawrence River on May 29, 1914, when the Norwegian collier the *Storstad* rammed its hull, killing 1,012 passengers and crew. In "The Wreck of the *Edmund Fitzgerald*," Gordon Lightfoot immortalized the 29 sailors lost aboard the doomed iron ore freighter, which went down in Whitefish Bay in Lake Superior on November 10, 1975. The massive oil rig *Ocean Ranger* went down in a storm in the Hibernia oil fields on February 15, 1982. All 84 hands were lost when the rig's lifeboat overturned in frigid waters. Thousands of other shipwrecks have occurred in our waters, forever changing the lives of the families of the lost sailors and passengers.

THE EASTERN GRAPHIC

The aftermath of the tidal surge, which ripped out sand dunes and pushed water over the causeway in Souris.

We live by the Charlottetown Harbour. Our house is close to the water, but we never thought that it would be something to worry about. The water had never come close before, so we weren't worried. During a tidal surge in January 2000, the weather had been nasty and the water was high. The water started rising towards our house, and it was pushing against the basement windows. There was so much pressure on them that they were pushed in with the water. My wife and I didn't worry too much until the water rose too high. We gathered some of the tools and various other objects from the basement. The water was rising too fast and we had to get out of the basement. The water rose so high that it put the furnace out and there was no heat in the house. The damage to our house was extensive.

Earl and Ruth Robertson,
as told to Rosalind Humphrey
Eastern Kings Consolidated School
Souris, Prince Edward Island

THE EASTERN GRAPHIC

THE EASTERN GRAPHIC

Back home now. My favourite jeans are safe, and my radio was upstairs during the storm since the one in the kitchen was broken. But the basement is a wreck. The water started to creep up the stairs, and little ice floes floated along the top. I was lucky compared to what happened to my cousin's cottage. It was blown into the water, and floated for a while, then gave itself a new place to stand.

from the diary of Kristin Cheverie
Eastern Kings Consolidated School
Souris, Prince Edward Island

On Friday, January 21, 2000, there was a tidal surge across Prince Edward Island. This tidal surge was caused by the way in which the earth, moon, and sun were in the same line. The high winds at that time made the water levels much higher than usual. With this gravitational pull being so powerful, the water surged over the land. There was a lot of damage to eastern P.E.I. Many roads were totally washed out and people had to drive around detours until the tide went down. The beach at Souris was greatly damaged. Many huge ice cakes washed ashore, removing much of the sand dunes that protected the causeway. The walkways at the beach were smashed and a lot of debris was left on the beach. There was also a lot of damage done to the wharf. People in western P.E.I. were forced to leave their homes. It was a busy night, as all fire departments, police officers, EMO, and the Coast Guard were at the scene to prevent further damage.

Tyler MacDonald
Eastern Kings Consolidated School
Souris, Prince Edward Island

In the far north, ice floes — chunks of ice of varying sizes — are a part of life, but they also pose a threat to the people of the region. Polar bears move from floe to floe hunting for seals. Hunters embark on hunting expeditions among the floes as well. When a floe breaks apart, or when the edge of the ice sheet breaks off into a floe, the consequences can be enormous. Hunting parties have become stranded upon the floes; in the north, where weather conditions are often treacherous, rescue operations are never easy.

The weather and geological phenomena take centre stage in these disasters. They are awe-inspiring, often beautiful, always furious. But it is the people in the disasters and the volunteers who rush to the scene who are the true heroes. Without the benevolence of these truly compassionate individuals, many more would find their lives and livelihoods threatened. The co-operation of various volunteer organizations, as well as the Canadian Forces and other government organizations, shows a spirit that is uniquely Canadian. Our country is beautiful, but often hazardous; we know what can happen, what will happen. We are more prepared than ever before to prevent disasters, or at least to diminish the harm done. If nothing else, we can warn people to get out of the way when there is no other alternative.

In 1954,
Hurricane Hazel
killed 83 people.
Big like a giant,
It blows winds of
100 kilometres an hour.
It has destroyed everything in its path,
homes and bridges.
In the darkness, the police,
the firefighters and the volunteers
Try to save it all.
They are all heroes.

Dusan Kneszevic and Gabriel Gervais Houle
Humewood Community School
Toronto, Ontario

In 1851, Elisha J. Baker was on board the ship *Abigail Gold*, which went down off the coast of Prince Edward Island during the Yankee Gale, an enormous storm. The sea tossed the ship; the timbers of the ship creaked and groaned. In one instant, crew members of the ship went to their watery graves. Elisha Baker survived the wreck.

Susan Leard
Eastern Kings Consolidated School
Souris, Prince Edward Island

THE EASTERN GRAPHIC

Souris Wharf, P.E.I.

Early on February 15, 1982, the ***Ocean Ranger***, the largest semi-submersible oilrig at that time, capsized and sank 166 nautical miles off Newfoundland during a horrific winter storm. It was the world's second largest offshore oil drilling disaster and Canada's worst marine disaster in decades.

The storm started as a small disturbance in the Gulf of Mexico on February 12. Two days later, it was located near St. John's and had a central pressure of 95.4 kPa. For most of that day, hurricane-force winds reaching 168 km/h and waves as high as 20 m had battered the rig. A list of 12 to 15 degrees developed port side, and in the early hours of February 15 the men abandoned the ***Ocean Ranger***. Soon after daybreak she slipped beneath the wild North Atlantic waters. Search-and-rescue crews battled zero visibility, freezing rain and snow, turbulent seas, and winds in their attempt to locate survivors. Any lifeboats that were found were unable to deal with the waves, and the men were tossed into the sea, where they either froze or drowned.

The storm also contributed to the sinking of Soviet container ship ***Mekhanik Tarasov***, which went down about 120 km east of the site where the ***Ocean Ranger*** sank.

Alex Helle

St. Patrick's Intermediate School

Ottawa, Ontario

In 1899, ice gathered about the abutments of the Honeymoon Bridge, spanning Niagara Falls, to a height of 80 feet, extending up into the steel work of the arch, bending it in places. The jam was so immense that gangs of men blasted away the ice on both sides of the Niagara River.

On January 23, 1938, a sudden windstorm off Lake Erie jammed the river with ice in 12 hours. The ice pushed against the supports, severely damaging them.

On January 27, 1938, the bridge crumbled. Experts blasted the wreckage of the bridge in sections. Portions of the bridge were lying at the bottom of the gorge. The arch laid on the ice broken in two pieces. The bridge stayed on the ice a long time. Tourists were attracted to the site during February, March and April, and finally in April, the bridge sank.

Although the bridge fell, nobody was hurt. The police placed signs and roadblocks around the downed bridge to stop people from driving into the river. Honeymoon Bridge had a spectacular funeral.

— Kirk Newton and Sean Frazer
Prince Philip Public School
Niagara Falls, Ontario

We are the only ones at North Lake,
so we are tense during the tidal surge
because one of the roads near our house
flooded. My little brother Chad came
running in saying, "Save the cat!
Save the dog! We're gonna die!
We're gonna die!"

"No, we're not," my mom said. "Go sit down." We all laughed but the situation was not funny.

If it had flooded more, it would have flooded our basement. Luckily the water went down in a couple of hours and we were okay — this time.

Tiffany Gregory
Eastern Kings Consolidated School
Souris, Prince Edward Island

PRIME MINISTER · PREMIER MINISTRE

It is with great pleasure that I extend my warmest greetings to the staff and volunteers of Construction Volunteers Canada on your Millennium book project, Children's Humanity in Large Disasters (C.H.I.L.D.).

This book, the proceeds of which will help to address the needs of our country's youth during natural disasters, will no doubt serve to inspire its readers. The stories, poems, photographs, and artistic work contained in its pages will enable us to better understand the devastating impact of catastrophic events and the important work carried out by those who volunteer to lend a hand to their communities and fellow citizens in times of need. All those involved in this project are to be commended for their commitment to Canada's young people; through this compilation, you are encouraging our youth to take an active role in their communities, while helping them share their experiences and insights with other Canadians.

Please accept my best wishes for every success in meeting your fundraising objectives.

OTTAWA
2001

PRIME MINISTER · PREMIER MINISTRE

Je suis heureux d'adresser mes plus cordiales salutations aux employés et aux amis de Bénévoles canadiens du bâtiment à l'occasion de la parution du livre issu du projet du millénaire ***Children's Humanity in Large Disasters****.*

Ce livre, dont les profits aideront à répondre aux besoins des jeunes en cas de catastrophe naturelle, saura sûrement inspirer ses lecteurs. Il contient des récits, poèmes, photographies et illustrations, qui nous permettront de saisir encore mieux l'ampleur des défis à relever et l'importance de l'assistance à offrir en cas de désastre. Toutes les personnes associées à ce projet méritent des éloges pour leur engagement envers la jeunesse; par ce livre, vous encouragez nos jeunes à jouer un rôle actif au sein de leurs communautés, tout en les aidant à partager leurs expériences et leurs vues avec les autres Canadiens.

Je vous souhaite bonne chance dans votre collecte de fonds.

OTTAWA
2001

Message from the Honourable Herb Gray, Deputy Prime Minister and Minister responsible for the Government of Canada's millennium initiative

Congratulations to Construction Volunteers Canada on the publication of a book depicting children's experiences during natural disasters.

Your organization is to be commended for the work you have accomplished since its inception following the 1998 ice storm, one of the worst natural disasters in Canada. The outpouring of compassion and help during that time was outstanding.

Children have very unique ideas about events that occur around them and this book is bringing that uniqueness to our attention. Their thoughts, their ordeals and their achievements, as well as their suggestions for survival techniques during disasters are shared with us in this wonderful book.

The Government of Canada is proud to support this project with a partial financial contribution through the Canada Millennium Partnership Program. Appearing as it does at the turn of the millennium, this book is sure to inspire readers to act in the spirit of our national millennium theme, "Sharing the Memory, Shaping the Dream."

Message de l'honorable Herb Gray, vice-premier ministre et ministre responsable de l'initiative du gouvernement du Canada pour le millénaire

Toutes nos félicitations aux Bénévoles canadiens du bâtiment pour la publication d'un livre illustrant les expériences vécues par des enfants lors de catastrophes naturelles.

Nous tenons à louer votre organisme pour le travail qu'il a accompli depuis sa création, à la suite de la tempête de verglas de 1998, l'une des pires catastrophes naturelles que le Canada a connues. Les manifestations de compassion et l'aide qui a été apportée durant cette période ont été remarquables.

Les enfants ressentent de façon très particulière les événements qui se produisent autour d'eux, et ce livre nous fait prendre conscience de cette particularité. Dans cet ouvrage remarquable, ces enfants nous livrent leurs pensées, leurs épreuves et leurs exploits, et nous proposent des méthodes de survie à utiliser en cas de catastrophe.

Le gouvernement du Canada est fier d'appuyer ce projet grâce au financement partiel accordé par le Programme des partenariats du millénaire du Canada. Publié ainsi au tournant du millénaire, ce livre incitera très certainement ses lecteurs à se comporter dans l'esprit du thème national que nous avons choisi pour le millénaire : « Des souvenirs à partager, des rêves à façonner. »

GLEN MURRAY
MAYOR • MAIRE

CITY OF WINNIPEG
CITY HALL
510 MAIN STREET
WINNIPEG, MANITOBA
R3B 1B9
(204) 986-2196
FAX: (204) 949-0566

VILLE DE WINNIPEG
HÔTEL DE VILLE
510, RUE MAIN
WINNIPEG (MANITOBA)
R3B 1B9
(204) 986-2196
TÉLÉC. : (204) 949-0566

WEB SITE/SITE WEB
http://www.city.winnipeg.mb.ca

December 19, 2000

Ms. Nancy Loewen,
61 Atlas Avenue
Toronto, ON
M6C 3P2

Dear Ms Loewen:

I Remember It Like Yesterday

Much has been written and recorded about the Manitoba Red River Valley Floods of 1997, especially the tremendous effort put forth by a great many people. As communities we were tested and challenged to succeed, by a river and other forces of nature.

The strength of resolve by our citizens in Winnipeg and in Southern Manitoba was remarkable.

As the rising Red River threatened Winnipeg, volunteers were desperately needed to assist residents building dikes to protect their homes. Thousands of volunteers put in many back-breaking hours throwing sandbags and constructing dikes. In fact, it is estimated there were 150,000 volunteer days of work contributed to the flood fight. The Volunteer Team arranged for services such as portable toilets, transit shuttles, and food for the volunteers. Organizations such as The Salvation Army and St. John Ambulance provided food, first aid, and other resources to the volunteers.

The City of Winnipeg actively planned, prepared for, and participated in the evacuation of the Red River Valley and from within Winnipeg. The primary activities included the registration, feeding, clothing, shelter, personal services and health services for more than 20,000 evacuees.

The key partners in assisting with the delivery of Emergency Health and Social Services are Recreation Services City of Winnipeg, Red Cross (registration and inquiry), Salvation Army (food), Provincial Health and Family Services (housing and

. . . . 2

-2-

personal services). In addition numerous volunteer organizations such as the United Way, Age and Opportunity Centre, and Meals on Wheels provided assistance, as did church groups, businesses and other associations.

The City prepared for the worst, including leaking dikes, dike failures, and the possibility the City would be hit by heavy rainfall. Public Works coordinated the construction of dikes (earth and sandbag) in flood stricken areas. City crews and volunteers filled over six million sandbags. If you put these six million sandbags end to end, they would stretch from Winnipeg to Vancouver.

Once the immediate danger had passed, the work was not over. The clean up was a massive job! The dikes had to be removed to prevent collapse of the riverbanks when water levels dropped. Again the call went out for volunteers, and again they responded, but not in the same numbers. People rightly changed their focus to assist those families and communities who fell victim to the river. The City later had to resort to large machinery to remove approximately five million sandbags.

The City of Winnipeg is enormously grateful to its civic employees, as well as students, the corporate community, community groups, thousands of individual volunteers, and the people from across Canada who came to our aid.

I encourage readers to log onto the City of Winnipeg web site at www.city.winnipeg.mb.ca/interhom/profile/flood/default.htm for full details on our experiences of the flood of 1997.

Sincerely yours,

Glen Murray,
MAYOR.

Cabinet du Maire

NATURAL CATASTROPHE

FLOOD OF JULY 1996

The people of Saguenay-Lac-St-Jean will not soon forget the flood of July 1996, an extraordinary natural catastrophe whose traces are still evident in the regional landscape today.

This disaster will have cost Canadian and Quebec citizens nearly half a billion dollars. This does not include the inestimable community mutual aid program set up during the first few days of the flood.

Without any particular request on the part of local municipal authorities who were overwhelmed by the scale of the disaster at the time, thousands of citizens throughout Canada, from New Brunswick to Vancouver, offered their spontaneous support to the victims of the 1996 flood. Hundreds of volunteer workers, including specialists in social work and all forms of mutual aid, joined hands in an unprecedented effort to help the thousands who suddenly found themselves homeless overnight.

The people of Saguenay-Lac-St-Jean know, more than any other Canadian today, the importance of volunteer work in our society. These workers of all ages, who are generous in serving their community with their time and life experience, continue to be important in this International Year of the Volunteer.

Therefore, I'd like to take this opportunity to transmit my deepest and most sincere gratitude,

Mayor Jean Tremblay

le mouvement de la rivière fait la joie de la ville

C.P. 129, Chicoutimi (Québec) G7H 5B8 - Téléphone : (418) 698-3023 - Télécopieur : (418) 698-3019
Courrier électronique : maire@ville.chicoutimi.qc.ca

Cabinet du Maire

CATASTROPHE NATURELLE

DÉLUGE DE JUILLET 1996

La population du Saguenay-Lac-St-Jean se souviendra longtemps du déluge de juillet 1996, une catastrophe naturelle exceptionnelle dont les traces de passage marquent encore aujourd'hui le paysage Saguenéen et Jeannois.

Un cataclisme qui aura coûté près de 1/2 milliard de dollars aux citoyens québécois et canadiens, sans compter le programme d'entraide socio-communautaire mis en branle les premiers jours du déluge, dont la valeur est inestimable.

Sans qu'aucune demande particulière n'ait été formulée par les autorités municipales en place, celles-ci étant débordées par l'ampleur de la catastrophe, des milliers de citoyens à travers le Canada, du Nouveau-Brunswick jusqu'à Vancouver, ont offert leur appui spontané aux victimes du déluge de juillet 1996. C'est ainsi que des centaines de travailleuses, travailleurs, bénévoles véritables spécialistes du travail social et de l'entraide sous toutes ses formes, se sont donnés la main dans un effort sans précédent, afin d'aider les milliers de sinistrés qui se sont retrouvés du jour au lendemain sans aucun bien ni logis.

Les Saguenéens et les Jeannois savent aujourd'hui encore plus que tout autre canadien et canadienne, l'importance du travail bénévole dans notre société, l'importance de ces travailleuses et travailleurs de tous les âges, généreux de leur temps et de leur expérience de vie au service de leur communauté en cette ***"Année internationale des volontaires"***.

Je profite donc de l'occasion qui m'est offerte pour leur transmettre mes profonds et sincères remerciements.

Le maire,

Jean Tremblay

JT/cg

le mouvement de la rivière fait la joie de la ville

C.P. 129, Chicoutimi (Québec) G7H 5B8 - Téléphone : (418) 698-3023 - Télécopieur : (418) 698-3019
Courrier électronique : maire@ville.chicoutimi.qc.ca

THE 1998 ICE STORM

The 1998 ice storm had devastating effects especially on the environment. The storm made us realize that Montréalers had strong ties of solidarity and that they could help each other in times of need.

The following are some of the lessons learned from this crisis:

• The need to anticipate the consequences of our decisions and actions

The fear was that if the temperature dropped, the situation would become catastrophic, and many more beds would have been required in the shelters. Colder temperatures would also have caused more serious damage to homes, businesses and industries. In fact the weather forecasters were alarmists in the middle of the week, when a cold snap was initially forecast.

• The need to consider citizens' expectations and to act upon them

We need to inform them about our own limits and to ask them to be self-sufficient if they can, for example, citizens should take toothbrushes, pillows, blankets, etc., to shelters.

The ice storm at one point, had transformed itself into a public work crisis, when citizens demanded fast results and were spurred by the media to have streets cleared, sidewalks cleaned and traffic flow restored.

Snow removal during the ice storm was complicated by the fact that the freezing rain stayed on the ground. Snow removal operations had to be stopped when only 30 percent of the city had been cleared and the operation had to be started from scratch since the major arteries, which are normally done first, had become impassable.

Twenty to thirty centimeters of ice covered every street and sidewalk. Cars stuck in the ice, branches, and in many places, household garbage, all combined to slow down snow removal and other operations

• The need to develop emergency plans for every crisis

It is a lot of work, I agree, and some of you may even think it is impossible but we need to invest in emergency preparedness planning and to try to use risk analysis to evaluate their consequences. The citizens expect their leaders to have anticipated the worst and expect them to have plans available for every situation, whenever needed.

• The need to direct and coordinate the involvement of volunteers

In general, volunteers who are organized are easier to work with, rather than with those that are spontaneous. In every good emergency plan, the contribution of volunteers is important. However, the ice storm taught us that it is hard to make effective use of everyone who wants to help out.

Structured volunteers: The structured volunteers, who are members of well-organized groups, are the easiest to mobilize when needed. They were very useful, particularly in the organization of shelters, in communications or in certain technical services jobs.

Spontaneous volunteers: We realized that it is difficult to provide leadership for spontaneous volunteers. We have to assess them, equip them and provide supervision for them, particularly if they are doing jobs in which they may get hurt, for which the city may be held liable.

There are also other points which are important to consider in times of crisis, for example:

- The need to use a field reconnaissance system to be better informed of each neighborhood's situation.
- The need to recognize the work done by our employees, of whom we demand a great deal.
- The need to be aware that employees are also victims of the disaster.
- The need to recognize that within shelters, the cohabitation between various groups can be difficult.
- The need to identify alternate suppliers. We had beds made, since the Red Cross could not keep up with the demand. We had production resumed in a bottled water plant. We hired lumberjacks from everywhere within the Province. In short, when a disaster of this magnitude occurs, all of the sources anticipated in our emergency plans are suddenly overloaded and we have to find goods and services elsewhere.
- The need to develop agreement for the exchange of services, manpower and equipment, even with smaller municipalities.

The extent of the disaster, affecting 660 of Quebec's 1,400 municipalities, made the supply of goods and services nearly impossible. The city's supplies services were extremely creative, and were able to unearth goods and services throughout northeastern North America. We acquired generators from the Gaspé, New Brunswick, Ontario, New York, Florida and Vermont area.

The need to establish ties with city administration and fire departments of similar size in order to receive assistance from them, if required, in a state of emergency.

Many states and cities have been helpful, all when contacted have assisted us within their capacity. Some have provided us with generators, heavy machinery equipment.

To conclude, we were ready, we had an emergency plan that we practiced and updated regularly. A plan that we had developed in consultation with all of the municipal departments. We acted, survived and learned from this crisis. All the time, effort and financial resources that we have invested in emergency preparedness have helped.

Pierre Bourque, Mayor

This inspirational and informative book is Construction Volunteers Canada's first charitable fundraiser. Book proceeds are primarily for youths' emergency needs in Canadian natural disasters. Youth in schools and adults representing various groups on a national scale have united in solidarity and in the "Canadian millennium spirit" for the purpose of writing this book. They have submitted photos, artwork, and historical articles depicting Canada's natural disasters. Most of the writers have experienced losses and traumas first hand either as a victim, volunteer, or donor because of natural disasters such as floods, tornadoes, or ice storms.

Nancy Loewen has written about her own personal experiences at disaster sites throughout Canada. She founded the non-profit construction charity in the height of the horrific Ice Storm of 1998. In an act of compassion, she appealed to companies and individual tradespeople across the country to donate material (lumber, carpeting, furniture, clothes, toys, appliances) and labour (truck operators, electricians, carpenters, plumbers, arborists) to relief efforts. Loewen and her tradespeople often travel great distances to the disaster sites.

The first copies of the book will be given to Prime Minister Jean Chrétien, the Honourable Herb Gray, and Governor General the Honourable Adrienne Clarkson. This project reinforces once again Canada's position as a leader in benevolence worldwide. Truly, Canadians are a compassionate and giving nation in times of adversity.

We believe this book will help alleviate fears of natural disasters because it focuses on the positive outcomes of natural disasters and the network of people in place to help suffering Canadians.

This book is a celebration of Canadian achievement and an exchange of reactions, interpretations, ideas, and approaches to restoring the lives of Canadians in the aftermath of natural disasters. It stresses the relevance of volunteerism, survival techniques, and coping strategies.

Unsung Heroes will most certainly contribute to the development of youth in a positive manner. Youth will meet adversity head on with courage and conviction, develop a respect for volunteers, see the kindness and generosity of many, and develop a better understanding of the power of nature.

Val Sterling
Marcella Hannah
Calgary, Alberta

Acknowledgements

The author would like to thank the following people and organizations for their support. Special mention to the media, who have supported our appeal for volunteer tradespeople, heavy equipment, vehicles, and materials. CVC is hoping to have a good working relationship with all Canadian media in the future.

Government

The Prime Minister of Canada, The Right Honourable Jean Chrétien
The Honourable Herb Gray
Millennium Bureau of Canada
Emergency Management Ontario (EMO)
Environment Canada (David Etkin)
Treasury Board of Canada
Geological Survey of Canada, Natural Resources Canada (Dr. Greg Brooks)
National Archives of Canada (Sophie Tellier)
Department of National Defence - Canadian Forces (Captain Bob Kennedy, Second Lieutenant (N) Luc Charron, Corporal Cindy Malano, Captain B. Barnett, Sergeant Serge Tremblay)
Health Canada
Ontario Ministry of Natural Resources, Aviation, Flood and Fire, Management Branch (Bob Thomas)
Ontario Ministry of Natural Resources, Forest Fire Management Centre (Debbie McLean, Dave Cleaveley)
Ontario Public Service
Office of Critical Infrastructure Protection and Emergency Preparedness
Prairie Farm Rehabilitation Administration (PFRA) Agriculture and Agri-Food Canada (Ken Burnett)
Solicitor General - Royal Canadian Mounted Police (RCMP) (Janice Burrow, Joanna Kerr, Dawn Seaman)

Police/Military

Ontario Provincial Police (Robert Rudd, editor, *OPP Review*; OPP Corporate Communications Bureau)
Metropolitan Toronto Police

Metropolitan Toronto Police Auxiliary

Air and Naval Reservists (Major Clifford Patterson, Lieutenant Christine Bazarin)

Maple Leaf (Canadian Forces Newspaper) (Mitch Gillett, Susan Turcotte, Ruthanne Urquhart, Kristina Davis, Anne Boys, Paul Mooney, Kevin Cowieson)

Garrison (Canadian Forces Newspaper) (Jon O'Connor)

Air Force Assocation of Canada

Schools

Ascension of Our Lord Secondary School, Mississauga, Ontario*

Richmond Regional High School, Richmond, Quebec*

St. Patrick's Intermediate School, Ottawa, Ontario*

Prince of Peace Catholic School, Borden, Ontario*

St. Joseph Catholic School, Prescott, Ontario*

Lindsay Place High School, Pointe-Claire, Quebec*

École W.S. Hawrylak School, Regina, Saskatchewan*

Hadley Junior High School, Hull, Quebec*

Ottawa-Carleton District School Board (Hyacinth Haddad)

Canadian Martyrs Catholic School, Oshawa, Ontario*

Nakasuk School, Iqaluit, Nunavut (the late Hal Richards)*

Lord Nelson School, Winnipeg, Manitoba*

St. Martin Catholic School, London, Ontario*

Chief Zzeh Gittlit School, Old Crow, Yukon*

Delburne Centralized School, Delburne, Alberta (Gabrielle Lamb)*

Humewood Community School, Toronto, Ontario*

The Good Shepherd Catholic School, Barrie, Ontario*

King Edward Public School, Peterborough, Ontario*

Peenamin McKenzie School, Sheshatshiu, Labrador*

Blessed Kateri Tekakwitha Catholic School, Orleans, Ontario*

Fairview Heights Elementary School, Halifax, Nova Scotia*

Huntsville Public School, Huntsville, Ontario*

**Denotes communities that will receive proceeds from the royalties of this book for use primarily for the needs of youth affected by natural disasters in Canada. Construction Volunteers Canada will determine those needs in cooperation with municipal officials.*

Academie Antoine-Manseau, Joliette, Quebec (Roger Desrochers)*
Byron Northview Public School, London, Ontario*
Holy Rosary Catholic School, Burlington, Ontario*
Morning Star Middle School, Mississauga, Ontario*
École St. Alphonse School, La Baie, Quebec (Steve Jansma)*
J.L. Jackson Junior Secondary School, Salmon Arm, British Columbia*
Range Lake North School, Yellowknife, North West Territories*
St. George Elementary School, Saskatoon, Saskatchewan*
Rideau Park School, Calgary, Alberta*
Queen of Peace School, Leamington, Ontario*
St. Jerome Catholic School, Hamilton, Ontario*
Prince Philip Public School, Niagara Falls, Ontario*
Hillsborough Elementary School, Hillsborough, New Brunswick*
St. Michael's Catholic School, Goose Bay, Labrador*
Nanook School, Apex, Nunavut*
Nasivvik High School, Pond Inlet, Nunavut (David Parks)*
Pond Inlet, Nunavut (Abbass Parks)
Eastern Kings Consolidated School, Souris, Prince Edward Island*
Waverley Elementary School, Vancouver, British Columbia*
Catholic Central High School, London, Ontario*
Queen's University, Kingston, Ontario (Stewart Fife)
University of New Brunswick, New Brunswick (Rob Blanchard)
University of Montreal, Quebec (Johanne Gelinas)

Municipalities

City of Montreal, Quebec (Mayor Pierre Bourke, 1994-2001)
Village of St-Valentin, Quebec (Jacquelyn and Yvon Landry, Diane and Yvon Fournier, René and Christine Trahan)
Ville de Chicoutimi, Quebec (Mayor Jean Tremblay)
Red Deer County, Red Deer, Alberta (Nancy Lougheed, Pauline Mousseau)
City of Winnipeg, Manitoba (Mayor Glen Murray, Cathy Chartier)

City of Toronto, Ontario (Bob Langmaid, Corporate; Ray Easby, Apparatus and Equipment, Fire; Norm Ferrier, EMS)

Organizations

Christian Reformed World Relief Committee of Canada (CRWRC) (Jacob Kramer)
Hydro-Québec (André Caillé)
Power One (Al Manchee, Olga Tirsalis)
Canadian Air Crane, Delta, British Columbia
Flying Tankers Inc., Port Alberni, British Columbia (Terry Dixon)
Al Miley & Associates, Professional Tree Care (Al Miley)
Home Depot Disaster Services (Ivana Vlcek)
Mennonite Disaster Service
Construction Volunteers Canada (Board of Directors)
Canadian Tire Foundation for Families
Radio Amateur of Canada (Pierre Mainville)
Ontario March of Dimes (Marsha Stephen)
Humane Society of Canada
Knights of Columbus, Ontario State Council
Canadian Red Cross
The Salvation Army, Emergency Disaster Services (Jim Ferguson, Jeff Noel)
The Women's Y of Montreal, Quebec (Andria Mallozzi)
The Perth Civitan Club (Robinson family)
Royal Canadian Legion, Dominion Command, Ottawa, Ontario (Ray Dick)
The Society of Saint Vincent de Paul (National Emergency Relief Committee, Ottawa Central Council)
Kinsmen & Kinette Clubs of Canada (Joseph Distel)
St. John Ambulance (National Headquarters of St. John Ambulance, Saint-Jean, Ottawa, Ontario; Julie Fenn)
Masons (Ted Morris, Masonic Lodge, Ontario; William T. Anderson, Masonic Grand Lodge, Ontario)
Junior Canadian Rangers (Captain Roger Archambault)
CLSC du Fjord, La Baie, Quebec (Sylvie Poirier)
Canadian Owners and Pilots Association, COPA, Flight 32 (Bill Nalepka)
Editors Association of Canada
Heidy Lawrance Associates
Friesens Corporation

Annex Publishing Ltd.
Hushion House Publishing Ltd.

Media and Magazines

The Weather Network (Karina Conley)
* *The Windsor Star*
* *Toronto Star Newspapers Ltd.*
* *National Post*
* *The Toronto Sun*
* *L' Express*
The Canadian Press (Anne-Marie Beaton)
* Canadian Broadcasting Corporation
* The Gazette
* The London Free Press
* *Leamington Post & Shopper* (Pat Bailey)
The Eastern Graphic, Montague, Prince Edward Island (Steve Fanning)
Red River Valley Echo, Altona, Manitoba
Better Farming — The Business Magazine for Ontario Agriculture (Robert Irwin)
Firefighting in Canada and Canadian Firefighter EMS Quarterly (Martin McAnulty)

Individuals

Joy Cummings Dickinson, New Brunswick
Marj Heinrichs, Rosenort, Manitoba
Frank Fitzmaurice, London, Ontario
Lynn Stegman, Red Deer, Alberta
Josh Stegman, Red Deer, Alberta
Barb Brouwer, Salmon Arm, British Columbia
Dr. Ivan H. Crowell, New Brunswick
The Wrights
Jane Christmas
Megan Bockus
Beth Crane
Andrea Kennedy
Allan Scudder
All the school principals and teachers who provided encouragement and guidance to students participating in this charitable project

*Denotes *media who have supported our charitable work in the past —our heartfelt gratitude for your support.*

Kinsmen & Kinette Clubs of Canada
Les Clubs Kin du Canada

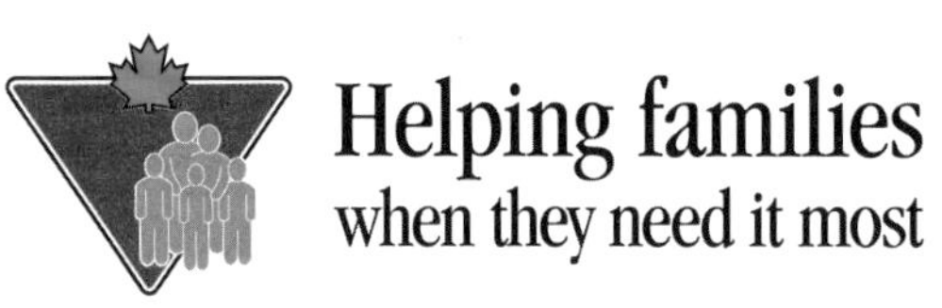

St. John Ambulance

CONSTRUCTION VOLUNTEERS CANADA
BÉNÉVOLES CANADIENS DU BÂTIMENT